THE AWESOME BOOK of BIBLE FACTS

How long would it have taken Mary and Joseph to drive to Bethlehem? page 58

What did Moses' basket and Noah's Ark have in common? page 14

What kind of fish did Peter catch with a coin in its mouth? page 62

Sandy Silverthorne

with Betty Fletcher

HARVEST HOUSE PUBLISHERS
EUGENE, OREGON

ADAM AND EVE

Genesis 1–3

IN THE BEGINNING, God created the world. On the sixth day, He made man from the dust of the earth. God placed him, fully grown, into a beautiul garden called Eden. There Adam, the first man, and Eve the first woman, lived happily. God often talked with them. Life was very good. That is, until the serpent tricked Eve into eating fruit from the only tree of which God had said, "Don't touch."

IF WE COULD TALK TO THE ANIMALS . . .

Some people believe that animals could talk in the garden. That would explain why Eve wasn't shocked when the serpent spoke to her. But after God told the serpent the consequences for tempting Eve, the old snake slithered away on his belly, never to speak again. He probably didn't waste any time either! Some snakes, like the black mamba of Africa, can travel up to 25 miles per hour.

ADAM'S APPLE?

Q: Why is that big lump on your throat called an "Adam's apple"?

A: Because that's where the fruit got stuck when Adam tried to swallow it!

Just kidding. People think the forbidden fruit was an apple, but the Bible doesn't say that. It could have been a peach, or even a pomegranate. The main thing is that Adam and Eve ate it. They didn't trust God to know what was best for them.

CLAY ART

Adam's name comes from the Hebrew word ă dā mâ, meaning "the ground." When God made Adam, He used many of earth's elements, including hydrogen and oxygen. Hydrogen and oxygen make water, and water makes up more than half your body weight.

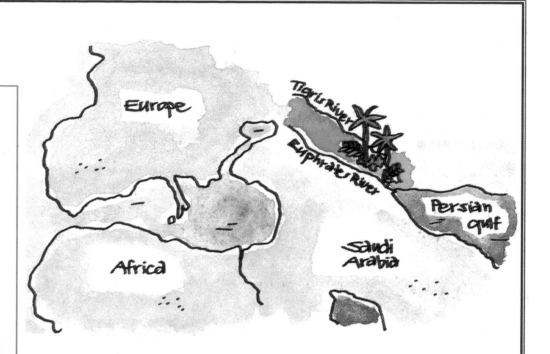

oxygen	.65%
carbon	.18%
hydrogen	.10%
nitrogen	.3%
calcium	.2%
phosphorus	.1.1%
other	.0.9%

A NICE GARDEN SPOT

Where was the garden? The Bible mentions four rivers near the garden of Eden. You can still find two of these rivers—the Euphrates and the Tigris (or Hiddekel)—on maps today. They are located near the Persian Gulf in Iraq.

NOAH AND THE ARK

Genesis 7–8

NOAH WAS A GOOD MAN. But he lived in a very wicked time—so wicked that God was sorry He had made people. For 120 years Noah tried to get them to turn back to God. They wouldn't. So God told Noah to build the ark. He sent the right number of every kind of animal to join him. Then the flood came. Everything that wasn't on the ark died. Afterward God gave Noah the rainbow as a sign of His wonderful promise never to flood the whole earth again.

AFTER ITS KIND

The Bible says that every kind of animal was on the ark. There were members of the cat family, the dog family, the horse family. But not every member of the family had to go.

HOW BIG WAS THE ARK?

The ark was about half the size of an aircraft carrier. Aircraft carriers are more than 1000 feet long and can carry 5000 people (and 90 planes). The ark was at least 450 feet long, 75 feet wide, and 45 feet high. It could hold as much cargo as 330 railroad cars!

1st year
2nd month
17th day flood starts

40 days and nights of rain

150 days

waters subside

7th month
7th day
Ark rests on Mt. Ara

SHIP AHOY! How long were Noah & Co. in the ark? If you guessed 40 days, you'd be wrong. (But nice try!)

SOMEWHERE OVER THE RAINBOW

Sunlight is made up of all of the colors of the rainbow. You see rainbows when the sun is behind you and the air in front of you is filled with mist. Water drops act like prisms, separating the sunlight into its colors. You can make a rainbow early in the morning or late in the evening by standing with your back to the sun and spraying water from a garden hose into the air.

smile everybody we want to remember this trip!

WATER, WATER EVERYWHERE

Most of us figure it just rained a lot, but Genesis 7:11 tells us that some kinds of earthquakes, tidal waves, or even undersea volcanoes added to the sudden, devastating flood. Where did all the water go? A lot of it ended up at the North and South Poles. Antarctica is covered by a solid sheet of ice up to 16,000 feet thick.

ALL ABOARD!

According to the Bible, there were eight people on this unusual voyage: 600-year-old Noah, his wife, their three sons—Shem, Ham, and Japheth (say that three times real fast!)—and their three wives.

After 7 days Noah sends out dove again

It returns with olive branch

10TH month tops of mountains are seen

After 40 days Noah sends out raven and dove

7 days later Noah sends out dove, it doesn't return

2nd year 1st month 1st day the ground is dry

2nd year 2nd month 27TH day family comes out

The rain poured down for 40 days, but it was a year and ten days before Noah's family was able to leave the ark.

TOWER OF BABEL

Genesis 11

SOMETIME AFTER THE FLOOD, some of Noah's descendants decided to build a tower. They wanted it to reach to the heavens to show how great they were. (They still hadn't learned that running their lives without God wasn't a good idea.) This didn't go over very well with God. So one day while they were building, God gave each of them a different language. The people were so confused that they gave up their big project and scattered all over the earth. They had wanted to make a name for themselves, but the only name they earned was "babblers"!

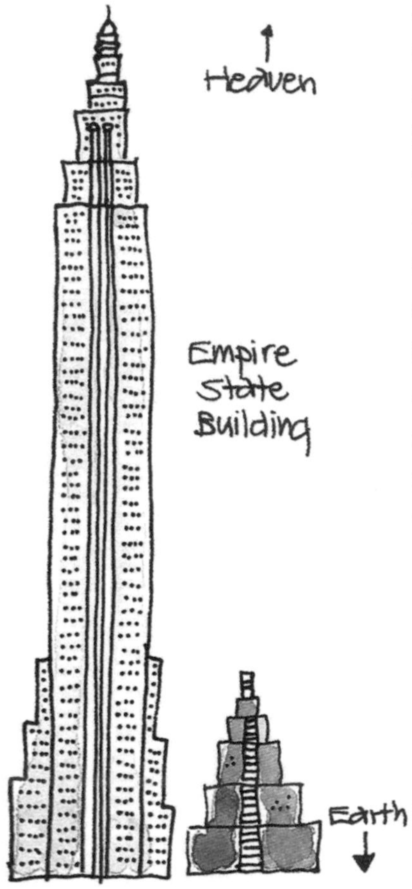

Heaven

Empire State Building

Earth

A ZIGGUR-WHAT?

The tower of Babel was probably a stair-stepped pyramid called a ziggurat. The tallest known ziggurat was about 300 feet high. That's tall, but hardly as high as heaven. It's not even as high as the Empire State Building, which is 1250 feet tall!

Got a delivery here for Babel!

Alá Asphalt

БЕРЕТИСЬ НИЖЕ НАС!

mao niy Katingalahan nga akong nakita...

Que cosé è?

Deze weg!

¿como?

ちがう こっちだ!

A SLIMY MESS

To build the tower, clay bricks were stacked on top of one another and held together with asphalt. Asphalt is a black, sticky tar that was found in ancient times and is still used in road-making today. In older versions of the Bible, asphalt is called "slime."

FRESH-BAKED DAILY

The bricks used in the ziggurats of Babylon were baked in an oven. They were flat and square. The ones made later in Egypt were dried in the sun and shaped like rectangles.

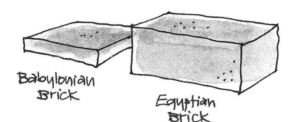

SPRECHEN SIE DEUTSCH?

Today there are more than 3000 different languages in the world.

ABRAHAM

Genesis 12–25

WHAT IF GOD SAID, "Pack up everything you own, say goodbye to your friends and country, and get ready for a long journey. I'll tell you when to stop"? That's what happened to Abraham! And you know what? He did it. That's one reason he's called the father of faith. He trusted God. God was leading Abraham to a land called Canaan. He wanted to bless Abraham by bringing him to this wonderful place. He also wanted to use Abraham to begin a great nation, the nation of Israel.

ROUTE 66

Once God led Abraham out of Ur (the country he lived in), Abraham and his caravan traveled through the "Fertile Crescent" along the Euphrates River. It is called the Fertile Crescent because everything grows well there and because it is shaped like a crescent moon!

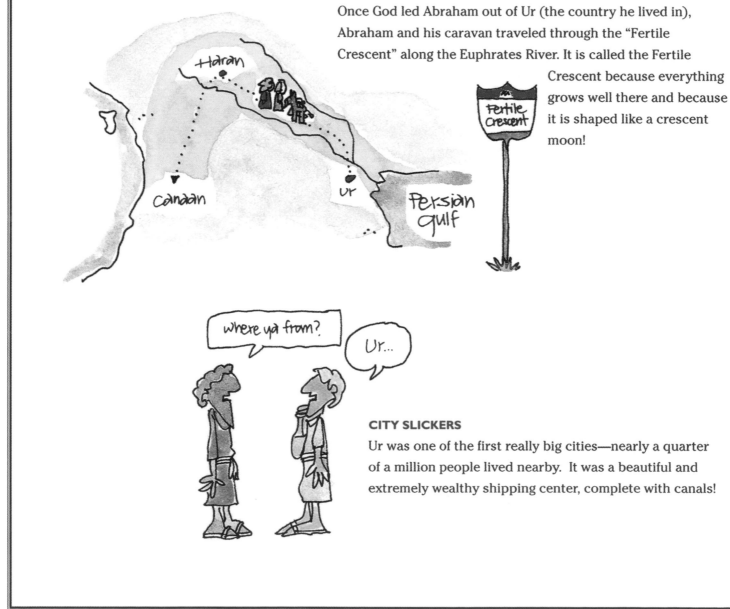

CITY SLICKERS

Ur was one of the first really big cities—nearly a quarter of a million people lived nearby. It was a beautiful and extremely wealthy shipping center, complete with canals!

MORE THAN THE STARS

The eye can see about 3000 stars in the sky. The number of Abraham's children, grandchildren, and great-great-really-great grandchildren through Isaac is many times that number—in fact, there are 18,000,000 Jewish people living today.

ABRAHAM'S TEST

The hardest time in Abraham's life came when God asked him to sacrifice his son, Isaac, on an altar on Mount Moriah. God had promised to make Abraham's children more numerous than the stars in the sky. But Isaac was the only son he and Sarah had! Abraham had faith. He believed that even if Isaac died, God would bring him back to life (Hebrews 11:18,19).

A TRUSTING SON

Isaac had faith too. He was probably between 16 and 25 years old. Abraham was more than 100. Isaac could have escaped easily. But he trusted his father and the Lord with his very life. And God came through—He provided a ram for the sacrifice at the very last minute.

DONKEY, DON'T YOU DALLY

Pictures of caravans usually show head-to-tail camels. But camels were just being tamed around Abraham's time (about 3000 years ago). Abraham used sturdy little donkeys to make the 400-mile journey.

PASS THE PEPTO

Abraham may have started his camel herd while visiting Egypt (Genesis 12:16). Camels were faster than donkeys. They could carry bigger loads—at least 400 pounds. And they could go for days without water. Only one problem—their swaying made people seasick.

JACOB AND ESAU

Genesis 25–33

THERE ONCE WERE TWO BROTHERS, twins named Esau and Jacob. Jacob's name meant "holding onto the heel" or "supplanter"—wrestling terms for gaining the advantage over an opponent. And that is just what Jacob did. He was even born grabbing his brother's heel! Jacob wanted to be first. The two brothers were as different as brothers could be. Esau, whose name means "hairy," was a rugged outdoorsman. He loved to hunt. Jacob was smooth-skinned and liked to stay close to home, taking care of the flocks. Their mother, Rebekah, favored Jacob, and their father, Isaac, favored Esau. . . and that's when the trouble began.

HOME ON THE RANGE

Isaac and his family were nomads. They lived in tents and moved from place to place when their livestock needed new pasture. A nomad's wealth was measured by the number of animals in his flock. Animals provided food and shelter and clothing. Isaac's family sometimes stayed in one place long enough to plant grain.

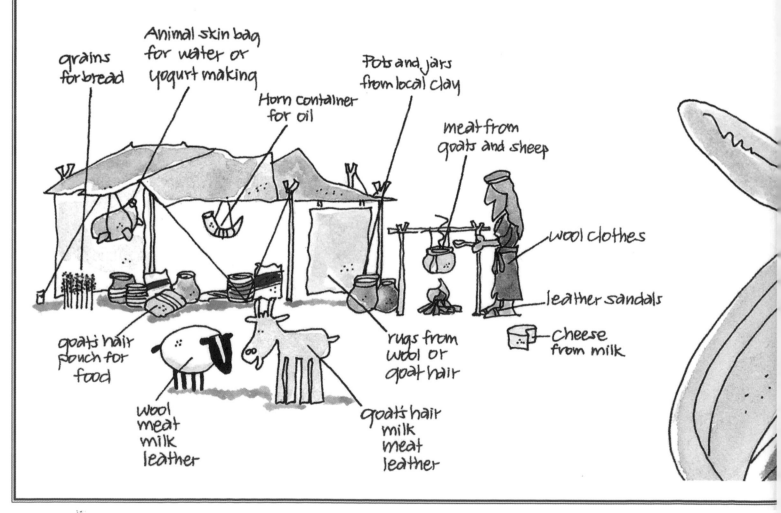

FOOD FIGHT

One day Esau showed up starving. "I've been hunting but had no luck. I'll give anything for a bowl of your home-cooked stew." Jacob seized his chance and traded the lentil stew for Esau's birthright. Birthrights were a very big deal in those days. The oldest son received twice as much inheritance.

THE STOLEN BLESSING

Just before he died, Isaac, who was now old and blind, asked Esau to go hunting for him one last time. Then he would bless him. But while Esau was gone, Rebekah put goatskins on Jacob's arms. Isaac thought Esau had returned and gave Jacob the blessing. Even though he had been tricked, Isaac couldn't take the blessing back.

ANGEL WRESTLING

For many years Jacob lived as far away as possible from angry Esau. But then God told him to go home. On the way, Jacob wrestled with an angel. As they wrestled, the angel gave him a new name. He would no longer be Jacob the trickster, but Israel, which means "God's fighter." Then the angel touched Jacob's hip (an unexpected move because it was below the belt), and dislocated it. Jacob was different after this. He stopped wrestling against people and became the father of the nation of Israel. He and Esau even made up!

BIRTHRIGHT STEW

Several handfuls of wild lentils, wild onions, salt, water, (meat optional)

Place in clay stewpot and allow to cook slowly over open fire. Stew is done when the broth turns red and the aroma is too good to resist.

JOSEPH

Genesis 37, 42–46

ONE DAY JOSEPH'S FATHER gave him a new coat. It made his brothers very jealous. Then Joseph had a dream. In his dream he and his older brothers were harvesting grain. The older brothers' stalks of wheat were bowing down to his stalks of wheat. This made the brothers angry. Who did Joseph think he was? They threw him in an empty water cistern and sold him to traders who were going to Egypt. The brothers tore up Joseph's beautiful coat and sprinkled goat's blood on it so their father would think a wild animal had killed Joseph. But God was with Joseph. He ended up working for Pharaoh, the great ruler of Egypt.

SALE TODAY!

When a caravan of traders from Midian passed by, the brothers saw their chance to make some money while getting rid of their pesky little brother. They sold Joseph for 20 shekels of silver— less than $50 today.

PLANNING AHEAD

Pharaoh put Joseph in charge of storing grain for the drought that was coming. After it arrived, Joseph's brothers became hungry. They went to Egypt to ask for food. Joseph forgave his brothers. Then all of Joseph's family moved to Egypt. Joseph said to his brothers, "You thought you were doing me harm by sending me to Egypt, but God used it to save your lives!"

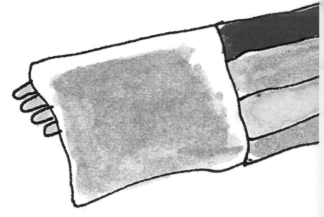

Hebrew

Egyptian

A NEW LOOK

At first Joseph's brothers had no idea that their little brother was the handsome Egyptian in front of them. Powerful men in Egypt dressed in a very stylish way. They shaved their beards and wore elegant headdresses and jewelry. These Egyptians also did something an Israelite man would never think to do—they wore makeup. No wonder the brothers didn't recognize Joseph!

THE PYRAMID CRAZE

Pyramids were a familiar sight to Joseph. But pyramid-building was only in fashion for 200-300 years. The pyramids Joseph saw had been standing for a thousand years by the time he arrived in Egypt.

HEAVYWEIGHT CHAMP

It took 2,500,000 blocks of stone to build the great pyramid of Cheops. The pyramid weighed in at about 5 *billion* pounds!

JOSEPH'S COAT

Sometimes words in other languages can mean more than one thing. Another possible meaning of Joseph's "coat of many colors" is "a long-sleeved tunic." In Joseph's day, people who did heavy work wore tunics that had short sleeves or no sleeves at all. Long-sleeved tunics were for people who didn't have to work hard!

SWEET DREAMS

God gave Joseph a special gift of understanding dreams. People normally dream about six times every night—even if they can't remember them!

BABY MOSES

Exodus 2

IN THE 300 YEARS AFTER JOSEPH DIED, his family in Egypt grew from 70 people to over 2 million. They outnumbered the Egyptians. The new pharaoh was afraid the Israelites might take over the land. He made them slaves and commanded that all Hebrew baby boys be put to death. It was during this time that Moses was born. To keep him alive, Moses' mother placed him in a reed basket and set it afloat in the Nile River. God saw to it that Pharaoh's daughter found him and adopted him.

NO PLACE LIKE HOME

Pharaoh's daughter needed a nurse for the baby. Unknowingly, she hired Moses' own mother to care for him until he was older. So Moses spent much of his early childhood with his birth parents. He never forgot his people.

ADVANCED PLACEMENT

In Pharaoh's palace, Moses received a prince's education. Princes were taught geometry, poetry, and astronomy. They learned to write in hieroglyphics and in other languages. Not many people knew how to write in those days. God was preparing Moses to write the first five books of the Bible.

תֵּבָה

The word used for Moses' watertight basket is the same word used for the ark Noah built. It means a floating vessel. Both arks were used to save a race of people, but in very different ways!

FIRE!

One day in Midian, Moses saw a burning bush—probably a mimosa or thorny acacia tree. It wasn't unusual to see a bush on fire in the desert. But there was something different about this bush. It burned, *but it didn't burn up!* God spoke to Moses there. He told Moses to go back to Egypt and tell Pharaoh to let His people leave. Moses was 80 years old!

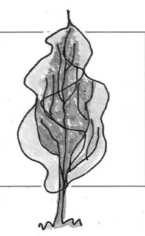

QUICK DRAW

When he was 40 years old, Moses had murdered an Egyptian who was beating a Hebrew. The next day he ran for his life to Midian, about 250 miles away. In Midian, Moses lived as a shepherd until God spoke to him from the burning bush.

PPPICK SSSOMEONE ELSSSE...

Moses told God that he wasn't a good choice to go to the new pharaoh (the old one had died) because he had a speech problem. But God didn't need someone who was perfect—just obedient. He sent Moses' older brother, Aaron, to help Moses.

PITHY PAPYRUS PRODUCES PAPER

We usually think that the bulrushes used to make Moses' boat were like little cattails. But they weren't. The three-sided reeds grew up to 16 feet tall and three inches across. Egyptians discovered how to make these plants into paper, sometimes in rolls 120 feet long!

THE PLAGUES

Exodus 7–12

D O YOU THINK MOSES' HEART WAS POUNDING when the guard called his name to appear before the ruler of the whole land? Moses knew that God was with him and his brother, Aaron. God had told Moses He was going to use him to free His people. But over and over Pharaoh's heart became hard. He wouldn't let God's people go. Even though Moses did many miracles, like turning his staff into a snake, Pharaoh wouldn't budge. Then God sent ten disasters called *plagues*. Finally, after the tenth and most horrible plague of all, Pharaoh said, "Go." And Moses led the people out of Egypt.

OPEN-DOOR POLICY

Moses had been a renegade shepherd in Midian for 40 years. Why did this new pharaoh let Moses talk to him? Despite his faults, Pharaoh sometimes let ordinary people come to speak with him. Unfortunately, Pharaoh didn't change very much as a result of the talks he and Moses had, but it was a good policy.

BACKBREAKING BRICKMAKING

The pharaohs used slaves to build new cities for them. First the people had to make bricks using mud and straw. The straw helped the bricks dry and made them stronger. While one man walked up and down in the mud and straw, others scooped it out and patted the wet mixture into a frame to harden in the sun. Then they carried the heavy bricks to the building site. A model that looks like this drawing was found in an ancient Egyptian tomb.

GETTING TO KNOW YOU

The plagues were a clear but painful way for Pharaoh and the Egyptians to get to know about the true God. The Egyptians worshiped many gods—gods of the river, of the sun, of the sky, of the crops. The ten plagues showed the Egyptians that the living God had more power than all of their so-called "gods" put together.

 **BLOOD.** God's first sign was that the Nile River turned to blood. The smell was unbelievable. Where was the river god?

 BOILS. These raised, burning bumps on the body were so painful that Pharaoh's magicians couldn't even stand up!

 **FROGS.** God sent so many frogs they were in everyone's beds, kitchens, and even their ovens!

 **HAIL.** This hail storm was mixed with fire. If you were caught outside in it, you died. Hail insulted Isis, the Egyptian goddess of life.

 **GNATS.** Do you say "g-nats" or "nats"? These tiny pests got under everyone's skin.

 **LOCUSTS.** These large grasshoppers had enormous appetites. They could (and still can) strip a land of all its crops in a matter of hours.

 **FLIES.** Besides being disgusting, swamp fly bites are painful. The Hebrews were spared this and the next three plagues.

 **DARKNESS.** This plague was important because the most powerful god in Egypt was the sun god, Ra. Pharaoh was supposed to be a human version of this god.

 **LIVESTOCK DISEASED.** All the cattle belonging to the Egyptians died.

 **DEATH OF THE FIRSTBORN—PASSOVER.** Only the Jews (and a few God-fearing Egyptians) who followed God's command to brush a lamb's blood over the doorpost of their houses escaped.

THE EXODUS

Exodus 13–40

AFTER THE TEN PLAGUES, Pharaoh let the Israelites go. Moses probably thought the battle was over, but in a way it was just beginning. Pharaoh changed his mind and sent his army and all his chariots to capture God's people. With the Red Sea in front of them and the enemy cutting off retreat, the Jewish people were trapped. But God is never trapped. He pushed back the waters of the Red Sea, and the people escaped! Then their desert journey really began.

ROLL CALL

Six hundred thousand men left Egypt. They took their wives and children, so about 2½ to 3 million people went with Moses. If all those who left were standing in a line, they would stretch from Egypt to the Promised Land and back!

Canaan

Egypt

ON THE ROAD AGAIN

God gave the people a pillar of fire by night and of cloud by day to guide them. There weren't two pillars—just one that changed from fire to cloud and cloud to fire.

COACH CLASS

The trip from Egypt to the Promised Land should have taken the large company of Israelites two to three months. Instead it took them 40 years.

I WANDER WHY?

Twelve spies had gone into the Promised Land. Joshua and Caleb told the people that it was a great place, and God would help them win victories there. The other ten spies told the people that Canaan had walled cities and armed giants and they would be killed. Because the people believed the bad report instead of trusting God, they had to wander in the wilderness.

DAILY BREAD

At first the Israelites didn't know what the small "seeds" that looked like frost were. So they named it "manna," which literally means "what?" in the Hebrew language. The manna stopped after the first Passover in the Promised Land.

ANYBODY HOME?

The Israelites were in the wilderness, but they weren't lost. Moses' father-in-law came all the way from Midian to visit Moses. He brought Moses' wife and two sons—and then he went home!

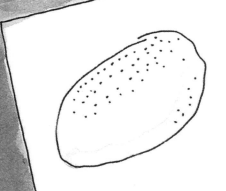

TODAY'S MENU
(Sorry, no substitutions)

MANNA~
Made fresh daily from heaven's finest ingredients, our manna cakes have the flakey pastry texture and honey-sweetened taste that you've loved for nearly 40 years!

QUAIL~
By special request. Spit-roasted to perfection over mesquite coals. Golden brown and crispy outside. Tender and juicy inside. All you can eat.

GOD'S GOOD RULES

I T'S SOMETIMES HARD TO UNDERSTAND why the Old Testament is so different from the New Testament. Just when you think God's people have learned to listen, they turn against Him again. Over and over God forgives them and helps them start fresh. But He also gives them very strict rules, like the ones He gave them after they left Egypt. And He punishes them when they do wrong—sometimes in ways that seem very harsh to us. Have you ever wondered about this?

AFTER-SCHOOL HELP

If you've ever needed help in arithmetic or spelling, you probably know what a tutor is. A tutor teaches you ways of learning things that you didn't know before. God's laws were like a tutor. They helped people learn what God was like and what things pleased Him.

BROKEN PROMISES

God's rules also helped the people see that they weren't perfect. They had promised to keep all of the laws, but they couldn't. God's rules helped them see that they needed a Savior.

THE CONDENSED VERSION

Q: Jesus said the whole law could be summed up in which two commands?
A: Love God with all your heart, soul, mind, and strength. Love people just like you love yourself.

IT MATTERS

How we live matters to God. He is perfect. He can't just turn His head when people do evil things. That's why Jesus came. When Jesus died, He took our punishment for the things we do wrong. That's the big difference between the Old Testament and the New Testament.

⬆ perfection

▬ us

Don't have any other go[d]
Don't make any idols f[or]
Don't take the Name of [God] in vain.
Remember to keep the S[abbath]
Honor your father and [mother]
Don't murder
Don't commit adulte[ry]
Don't steal
Don't lie
Don't covet other pe[ople's]

ONE, TWO, OR FOUR?

After Moses led the people out of Egypt, God gave His people the Ten Commandments. They were an agreement between them. When a strong king made an agreement with a weaker nation, he wrote out two copies of the covenant, one for himself and one for the people. God gave Moses both copies to show Israel that He was right there with them. When Moses came down the mountain and saw the people worshiping a golden calf, it made him angry. He broke both copies. Later God wrote two more, so there were four copies of the Ten Commandments.

THE LAST SHALL BE FIRST

People think it would be neat to have seen Jesus. But Jesus said that people who haven't seen Him and still believe in Him are special. He promised to bless them (John 20:29).

SOFT HEARTS

The law was written on tablets of stone, but Jesus puts it in our hearts instead. He gives us soft hearts instead of hard ones so that we can understand Him.

before me

r yourself

ne LORD

bbath day

nother

)

ple's things

Don't have any gods before me

Don't make any idols for yourself

Don't take the Name of the LORD in vain.

Remember to keep the Sabbath day

Honor your father and mother

Don't murder

Don't commit adultery

Don't steal

Don't lie

Don't covet other people's things

JOSHUA

Joshua 1–11

AFTER MOSES DIED, JOSHUA BECAME THE NEW LEADER. It must have been scary trying to fill Moses' sandals because three times God had to remind him, "Be strong and courageous." Joshua led the children of Israel into the Promised Land. Once there, they were supposed to capture all the cities. But it was the season for floods. How could they cross the Jordan River? God told Joshua to tell the priests to step into the river with the Ark of the Covenant. As their feet touched the water, the river stopped flowing. They walked over on dry ground. Nobody from Jericho expected invaders from the east during flood season!

DIRTY DEAL

In 1927, some earth tremors caused dirt to block the Jordan River in just about the same place. It was stopped up for more than 20 hours!

COME ON DOWN!

Jesus was visiting Jericho when he called Zaccheus down from his tree.

STAKEOUT

Joshua sent spies into the city of Jericho. They went to the house of Rahab, a woman of questionable character. She knew that Israel's God was true, so she helped the spies. In return, they helped her family escape. Why did spies check out the city when God already knew He was going to cause the walls to fall down? God wanted to save Rahab.

A REAL OLD TOWN

Jericho is the oldest walled city in the world. In Joshua's time it wasn't large (about eight city blocks), but its long history and strong, thick walls made it seem invincible.

mine

DON'T TOUCH THAT!

Joshua put Jericho "under the ban." No one was to take any loot from their first conquest. But Achan smuggled out a Babylonian garment, 200 shekels of silver, and a wedge of gold. Because he disobeyed, the Israelites were defeated in their next battle at the city of Ai.

Hazor was a powerful, fortified city on the main trade route between Mesopotamia and Egypt. This was a great victory for Joshua's army.

sea of galilee

Joshua planned an ambush. The army of Ai rushed out, feeling confident after its earlier victory. But 30,000 Israelites sprang from their hiding places and burned the city.

Joshua prayed. God made the sun stand still.

At Jericho, the trumpets blew, the Israelites shouted, and the walls fell down.

The Gibeonites tricked Joshua into making a treaty. They dressed in dirty old clothes and claimed to have come from a far country. Really, it was only 20 miles!

God dried up the Jordan River. Joshua built a monument with stones from the middle of the river.

The Lord sent killer hailstones down on the Canaanite army.

Joshua and his army quickly took over all of these smaller cities. The southern portion of the land belonged to Israel!

Libnah

Lachish

Eglon

Hebron

Debir

Dead Sea

WINNER TAKES ALL

The Israelites rarely destroyed cities. Instead they moved into the existing homes. This fulfilled God's promise that they would live in cities they hadn't built.

A PEOPLE SET APART

God commanded Joshua to kill every person who lived in the land of Canaan. Why? Because whenever the Israelites married people who did not know the living God, they began to worship other gods.

AWESOME OLD TESTAMENT FACTS

OLD TESTAMENT PROPHET WHO ATE A BOOK IN A DREAM

Ezekiel

THE SIX EARLIEST INVENTORS

1. Abel: shepherding (Genesis 4:2)

2. Cain: farming (4:2); cities (4:17)

3. Jabal: tents (4:20)

4. Jubal: harp and organ (4:21)

5. Tubal-cain: metal-working (4:22)

6. Noah: wine (9:20,21)

FOUR BALD MEN IN THE OLD TESTAMENT

1. Samson: Delilah shaved his hair (Judges 16:19)

2. Elisha: naturally bald (2 Kings 2:23)

3. Ezra: plucked out his own hair and beard (Ezra 9:3)

4. Job: shaved his head (Job 1:20)

THE FIVE HAIRIEST MEN IN THE OLD TESTAMENT

1. Esau: a "very hairy man" (Genesis 27:11-22)

2. Elijah: a "hairy man" (obviously not as hairy as very hairy Esau!)

3. Samson: the Nazarite

4. Absalom was so proud of his long hair he had it cut only once a year. It weighed 200 shekels—about five pounds (2 Samuel 14:26).

5. Nebuchadnezzar (a king in Daniel's time): His hair grew like eagles' feathers (Daniel 4:33).

TWO TIMES THE SUN LOST TRACK OF TIME

1. When Joshua prayed, the sun stood still for nearly a day (Joshua 10:12,13).

2. The Lord confirmed his promise of healing to Hezekiah by having the sun reverse its direction. The shadow on the sun dial moved back ten degrees (2 Kings 20:8-11).

LONGEST BOOK IN THE OLD TESTAMENT

Psalms:150 chapters

SHORTEST BOOK IN THE OLD TESTAMENT

Obadiah: 21 verses

THE JUDGES

URING THE PERIOD OF THE JUDGES, beginning about 1375 years before Christ, the nation of Israel was in chaos. The people had been led to the Promised Land by strong leaders like Moses and Joshua, yet they had no human king. The living God was their king. But they had trouble obeying a king who could not be seen. Soon everyone started doing what he or she wanted. The people ignored God and His commandments.

Because they were rebellious, enemies like the Philistines, Midianites, and Ammonites made life miserable for them. When the trouble grew bad enough, the Israelites cried out to God. God always heard and sent "judges" or "deliverers" to save them from their misery. Deborah, Gideon, and Samson were three such deliverers.

JOB SECURITY

God chose the judges. They were given the job for life, just like the judges on our Supreme Court!
The judges ruled over Israel for about 300 years.

JUDICIAL TRIVIA
Q: What were the names of the first and last judges of Israel?
A: Othniel and Samuel.

DEBORAH

Judges 4–5

DEBORAH WAS A ONE-OF-A-KIND WOMAN. She is the only woman judge mentioned in the Bible. She was a prophetess. She led an army to war. And she was a songwriter too! (She wrote one of Israel's all-time classics...but more on that later.)

YOU OLD STICK-IN-THE-MUD

A prophet or a prophetess was someone God used to tell his people what was going to happen in the future. Deborah told the captain of the army that the Lord was going to give God's people victory in a battle. But the other side had 900 iron chariots—and they had none! Captain Barak wouldn't take his army out to fight unless Deborah led them. So she did. The Lord sent a torrent of rain. All of the chariots got stuck in the mud. And Deborah's army won!

rats

may it please the court...

ROOM WITH A VIEW

Deborah set up her judging offices under a palm tree in the hilly country of Ephraim. People came to her with their problems, and God helped her judge wisely between them.

AMAZING PROPHECIES

Prophecies were sometimes given to encourage people. Many times they were given to reveal God's unfolding plan to bring people back to Himself. More than 100 different prophecies (about 300 counting repeats) in the Old Testament tell about the coming of Jesus or give specifics about His life. Every one of them is fulfilled in the New Testament. Here are just a few:

Given	PROPHECY	Fulfilled
Isaiah 7:14	Born of a virgin	Luke 1:34
Micah 5:2	Birth in Bethlehem	Mathew 2:1
Hosea 11:1	Live in Egypt for a time	Matthew 2:14,15
Zechariah 9:9	Enter Jerusalem on donkey	John 12:14,15
Psalm 22:16-18	Crucifixion	Luke 23:33
Psalm 16:10	Rise from the dead	Mark 16:6

GREATEST HITS OF 1200 B.C.

Deborah's song celebrates the victory that the Lord gave His people in the battle. It is one of the oldest Hebrew poems. One beautiful line says, "The stars fought from heaven, from their courses they fought against Sisera." God was on the Israelites' side. Afterward, there was peace in the land for 40 years.

ISRAEL'S TOP TUNES

#1 *Deborah's Song*
"Let those who love Him be like the rising of the sun in its might."

#2 *The Song of Moses*
"The Lord is my strength and song, and He has become my salvation."

#3 *Miriam's Song*
"Sing to the Lord, for He is highly exalted."

#4 *Song of Solomon*
"How beautiful you are, my darling, how beautiful you are!"

GIDEON

Judges 6–7

Gideon lived about 1100 years before Jesus was born, in a time when Israel was terrorized by an enemy from the east, the Midianites. Every time the Jewish people tried to harvest their crops, the Midianites rode in on camels, stole the grain, and beat up the farmers. They acted like school bullies. The angel of the Lord came to Gideon and told him God was going to deliver Israel. So Gideon gathered an army of 32,000 (quick recruiting) and headed off to fight the Midianites. But there were too many men for God. Gideon might think that *he* had accomplished the victory. So God slimmed down the forces, first to 10,000 and then to 300!

MIGHTY MAN IS ON HIS WAY...

When the angel found Gideon, he was threshing wheat in a wine press. Wheat is supposed to be threshed on a hill, and a wine press is a big hole in the ground used to tread out the grapes. Gideon was hiding from the Midianites. It must have surprised him when the angel called him a "mighty man of valor"!

Right Way

wrong way

SHREDDED WHEAT

To thresh wheat, workers tossed the grain into the air on a pitchfork. The heavy wheat kernels (good stuff) fell to the ground while the hollow shells or chaff (bad stuff) blew away. That's why threshing was done on a windy hill—there's not much breeze in a wine press!

Army Roster

ENCOURAGE ME!

Gideon needed assurance from God, so he laid a sheepskin on the ground. He asked God to make the fleece damp and the ground dry by morning. That was just what happened. "Could You possibly make the fleece dry and the ground wet this time?" Gideon asked. This would really be a miracle because the ground usually dries faster than wool. The next morning the ground was wet and the fleece was dry. God gave Gideon the encouragement he needed.

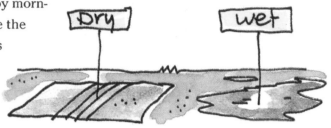

A WOOLY EXPERIMENT

Take a wool baseball cap out on the lawn on a sunny day. Wet the cap and the ground and see which dries first!

Who goes there?

glug glug

Figure 1

Figure 2

FRAIDY CATS, GO HOME!

To trim his army down, Gideon let everyone who was afraid go home. He took the remaining 10,000 men to a stream and told them to drink. 9700 of them drank from their knees, while 300 lapped the water from their hand. A man getting down with his face in the water would be open to attack. The valiant 300 stayed alert. Gideon took those 300 men.

MIDNIGHT SURPRISE

Gideon gave each man a trumpet, a torch, and a pitcher. On his signal, each man broke his pitcher, exposing the torches, and blew his trumpet. Most battles occurred in the daytime on a battlefield, so the Midianites thought they were about to get slaughtered in their tents. They ran in every direction!

DRUM AND BUGLE CORPS

Armies usually had only one trumpeter for every company of men. When the Midianites heard 300 trumpets, they thought there were 300 companies of Israelites. No wonder they were scared!

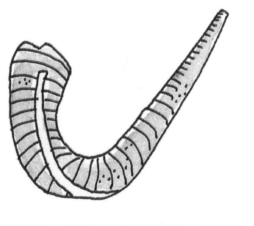

SAMSON

Judges 13–16

SAMSON WAS ONE OF ISRAEL'S GREATEST ALL-AROUND ATHLETES. He was so strong, he once took out 1000 of Israel's enemies with the jawbone of a donkey! Before he was born, an angel announced that he was to be a Nazirite—someone who was dedicated to God. God had great plans for Samson. He was to help deliver his people from the Philistines. But Samson began to go his own way. He broke his Nazirite vows and was captured by his enemies. Yet because he was sorry, even as a prisoner, Samson was used by God. God gave him back his strength one last time. Samson pushed against the stone pillars and the temple walls came crashing down, killing 3000 Philistines.

BIG HAIR

How long was Samson's hair? The world record for long hair is 12 feet 8 inches. Hair grows about half an inch every month (but usually maxes out at three feet). Samson was 20 years old, so his hair *could* have been as much as ten feet long! Samson braided his hair into seven locks. Still, it would have been tough to fit under a baseball cap!

crossbeam

doors

frame

hinges

Samson

POWER LIFTING

Once when Samson heard that the Philistines were planning to ambush him, he got up at midnight and went to the city gate. This was no ordinary garden gate. It was huge! He pulled out the gateposts, crossbars, metal hinges, and all and hiked with them on his shoulders to the top of a hill! Gates represented a city's security. Samson was showing the Philistines that someone with God on his side was stronger than a whole city.

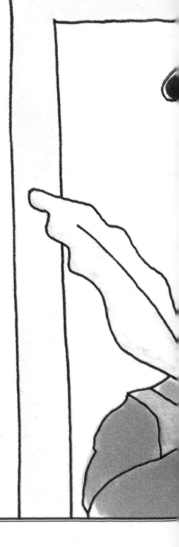

THE NAZIRITE VOW

No wine or
strong alcohol

No touching
dead stuff

No haircuts

Samson

CAREER STATS

Age drafted: before birth

Agent: an angel

Team: Nazirites

Age called up to the big leagues: 20

Years in the pros: 20

Position: pitcher

Total strikeouts: over 4000

Batting average: 1.000

Favorite bat: donkey's jawbone

Major strength: hair

Major weakness: Delilah

RUTH

Ruth 1–4

DURING THE PERIOD OF THE JUDGES, there was a devastating famine in Israel. A Jewish man named Elimelech, his wife, Naomi, and their two sons fled southeast to Moab to escape. While there, Elimelech and his sons died. When Naomi returned to Israel, her daughter-in-law Ruth, who was a Moabite, came with her. They were alone and poor, so Ruth started cutting barley from the field of one of Naomi's relatives. Soon the relative, a good man named Boaz, fell in love with and married Ruth. What had begun in heartache ended with joy and celebration.

CUTTING CORNERS

Ruth was able to cut grain from the corners of Boaz's field because years before God had commanded landowners to harvest only the middle portion of their property. Poor people could then come and gather or "glean" what was left. This was an early way of caring for the less fortunate.

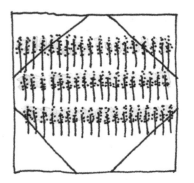

BRINGING IN THE SHEAVES

Ruth cut all of her grain by hand and tied it into bundles called "sheaves." Today machines known as combines can do all of the work!

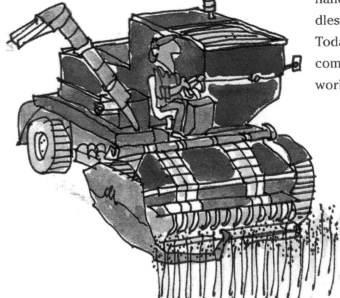

KINSMAN-REDEEMER

When a husband died in Ruth's day, God had a plan to take care of the wife. He commanded the man's brother (or nearest relative) to marry and support the widowed woman. This man was called the *kinsman-redeemer*. Boaz was a relative of Elimelech, so he acted as Ruth's kinsman-redeemer.

HERE'S MY SANDAL...

In ancient Israel, giving your sandal to another person was a way of making an agreement legal. The custom probably started because God had promised His people, "Every place on which the sole of your foot shall tread shall be yours" (Deuteronomy 11:24).

AN IMPORTANT MEETING PLACE

Boaz wanted to marry Ruth, but there was another relative who was closer than he was. He needed to make an agreement with that man. The two men met at the city gate. In those days the city gate was the place where important matters were decided, often in front of the town leaders.

COME ONE, COME ALL

Although Ruth was not an Israelite, she became the great-grandmother of King David and joined the royal bloodline of Jesus by marrying Boaz. This was to show us that God welcomes all who want to join His family, no matter what their background.

BATTLE PLANS

THERE WERE MANY WAYS TO WAGE war in Bible times. In the battle that Deborah led, large numbers of soldiers met in an open battlefield and fought hand-to-hand. The Babylonians captured cities by storming their walls. Occasionally, armies would choose one man from each side to fight and decide the whole war (like David and Goliath). Or one army would sometimes lie in wait to ambush another, as Joshua's army did at the city of Ai. It took great strength and courage to fight at such close range.

THE THREE CHARIOTEERS
Israelite chariots carried three soldiers: a driver, an officer, and a warrior.

BIG-TICKET ITEM
Chariots were expensive! A chariot was worth more than a man. Joseph was sold for 20 shekels of silver, but King Solomon paid 600 shekels—about $1300 today—for each of his 1400 chariots!

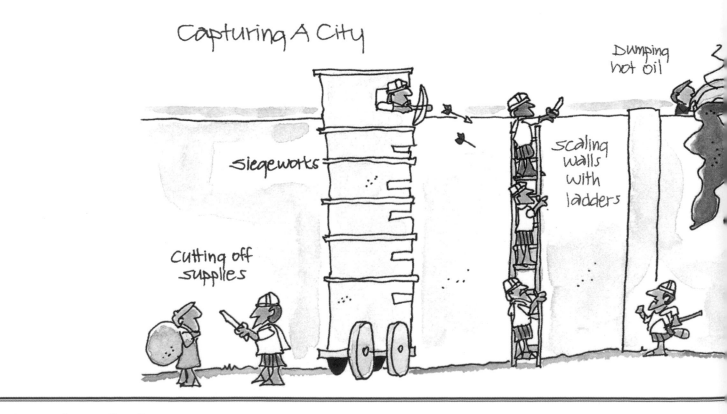

Capturing A City

Siegeworks

Dumping hot oil

scaling walls with ladders

Cutting off supplies

TRIBUTE

Sometimes one country would pay a stronger country not to attack it. This payment was called "tribute." Sometimes tribute was gold or silver, but often it was cattle, grain, and other produce from the land.

ALL AQUIVER

A quiver, the pouch that held an archer's arrows, held about 30 arrows. Arrows from Old Testament times have been found with their owner's name engraved on them!

YOU'RE IN THE ARMY NOW

The largest army in the Bible had 1,000,000 men. Commander Zerah from Ethiopia (a country in Africa) picked a fight with King Asa of Judah (the southern part of Israel). King Asa's army had less than half the men of Commander Zerah's, but the army from Judah won because God was on its side.

DEFENSE

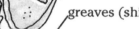

helmet

coat of mail

shield

greaves (shin guards)

Hurling stones

Throwing torches

Archers

Breaking the wall with a battering ram

Digging beneath the walls

Attacking the gates with axes and fire

DAVID AND GOLIATH

1 Samuel 17

THE STORY OF DAVID AND GOLIATH is one of the most famous in the Bible. But how tall was Goliath? And how did a young shepherd boy defeat him with a slingshot? Whoa, this is an amazing story! David trusted God to help him beat the boastful giant who was saying terrible things about God's people.

THE SLING

David's sling wasn't like our modern slingshots. It was a small leather patch with two long straps. After placing a rock in the patch, the shepherd would hold both straps and swing the sling over his head. When he let go of one of the straps, the stone would zing out at more than 60 miles an hour! A sharp-shooting shepherd could hit a target 50 yards away.

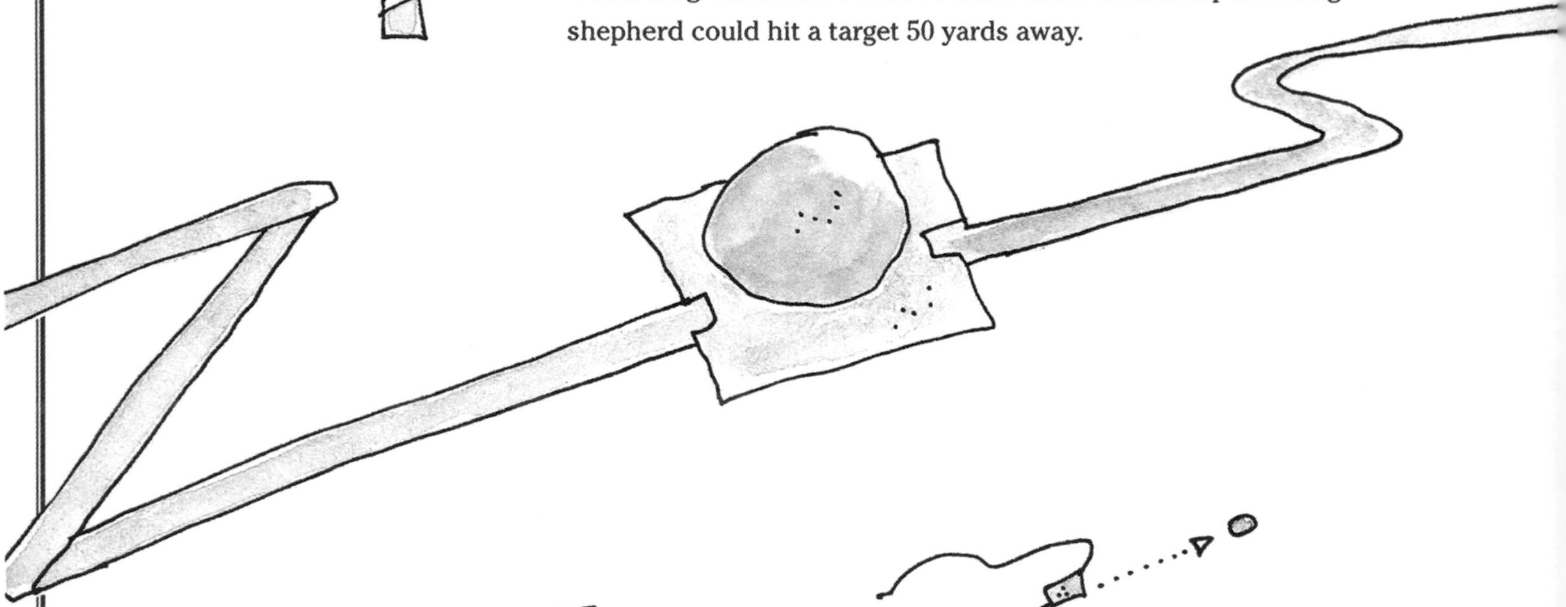

figure 1

figure 2

David!!

Do Not try this at home

COULD GOLIATH PLAY IN THE NBA?

Though 1 Samuel 17:4 says Goliath measured "six cubits and a span," we're not exactly sure how tall he was. If a cubit was 18 inches, that would make Goliath 9' 9" tall. Some people believe a cubit was 21 inches, and that puts him over the 11-foot mark! Either way, Goliath was one big dude! Considering the average NBA center is around 7 feet tall, Goliath and his four giant relatives (2 Samuel 21:15-22) would have made a terrific starting lineup. There's no height limit in professional basketball, but Goliath would have had to watch his mouth. Two technicals and you're outta there!

10ft.

7ft.

PHILISTINE ARMY SURPLUS

The weapons Goliath carried were big, too. His coat of bronze mail weighed 126 pounds—about as much as your Aunt Ethel—and the head of his iron spear weighed 16 pounds. And that's not counting his bronze shin-guards and heavy-duty helmet.

DAVID'S DIARY

KING DAVID WAS A WARRIOR, but he also loved writing his deepest thoughts to God. Hey, you can be strong and still feel things. Some of David's psalms were written early in his life. He probably wrote his most famous psalm, Psalm 23, while he was still a shepherd boy. As he watched over his flock, David saw how God takes care of His people like a good shepherd takes care of his sheep.

Have you ever wanted to read someone else's diary? That's what these psalms are like. Here's a peek. . .

PSALM 59

HELP!

David wrote this when he was on the run after escaping from Saul's palace. Saul was jealous of David and wanted to kill him. But David escaped, saying, "God is my defense."

PSALM 56

HE'S THE ONE!

David ran to the land of the Philistines to hide from Saul. He didn't think anyone would recognize him. But David had killed Goliath, who happened to be a Philistine. Nobody had forgotten that! David was scared and wrote to the Lord, "When I am afraid, I will trust in You."

PSALM 34

YOU GOTTA BE CRAZY

All David could think to do was to act so crazy the Philistines would leave him alone. He drooled. He scratched at the walls. It worked! So David thanked God for rescuing him. He wrote, "I sought the Lord, and He heard me, and delivered me from all my fears."

PSALM 52

THE GOSSIP

Doeg the Edomite (yep, that's his name) told Saul about David's visit to the temple in the town of Nob. Because he tattled, all the priests in the temple were killed. No wonder David wrote, "Your tongue devises destruction."

MUSIC MAN

The word "psalm" means "song"—usually accompanied by instruments. David introduced many musical instruments into Jewish worship.

• First instruments mentioned in the Bible: lyre and pipe.
• Biggest band: 4000 musicians served in the temple in David's time.
• Number of singers in trained temple choir: 288.

BE YOUR OWN PSALMIST

Why not start a prayer journal like David? Write to God. Tell Him about the things that are hard for you and the things that make you glad. Ask Him to help you. Then when your prayers are answered, go back and write how God answered them. You will be surprised!

PSALM 7

DON'T TOUCH GOD'S MAN

Twice, David could have killed Saul. But David chose to trust God with his future and not strike the man who was the leader of God's people. So when Cush accused David of treachery against the king, David said to the Lord, "If I have done this. . . let the enemy pursue my soul and overtake it." David knew he was innocent.

PSALM 51

THE NOT-SO-GREAT COVERUP

As king, David did many great things for Israel. But when he grew older, he sinned and took another man's wife, Bathsheba. To hide his sin, he arranged the murder of her husband. He couldn't hide from God, though. Afterward David prayed, "Create in me a clean heart, O God."

PSALM 3

SAD DAD

In David's later years, his son Absalom plotted against him. *He* wanted to be king. Rather than fight his own son, David left Jerusalem. This psalm was probably written as David journeyed from the city.

PSALM 30

LOOKING BACK

This psalm reflects David's thanksgiving for God's faithfulness throughout his life. It always seems easier for us to look back and see God's hand in things past than in things we're going through now. David's diary teaches us the importance of trusting, asking, and thanking God in all our circumstances.

SOLOMON'S BEAUTIFUL TEMPLE

1 Kings 5–8

WHEN DAVID WAS OLDER and the land was peaceful (yes, he got his kingdom back!), he wanted to build a temple for the Lord. This pleased God. But God told David that his son Solomon should be the one to build it. As the time drew near for Solomon to become king, David began preparing for the Temple's construction. God gave David a plan for the building, which he passed along to his son. David also arranged for wood and workers from his friend Hiram, king of Tyre. Solomon was happy. He couldn't wait to begin!

THE HOLY PLACE

This beautiful gold-plated room held an altar and a table of "showbread." The showbread was actually 12 loaves of bread that the priests were allowed to eat only in the sanctuary. New bread was put out every week.

THE HOLIEST PLACE

The innermost chamber of the Temple was separated by a beautifully woven curtain. The Holy of Holies was where the Ark of the Covenant rested. When the Temple was finished, God filled this room with His special presence. (After Jesus died for our sins, God sent His Holy Spirit to live inside each believer. Now God's presence fills *us* instead of a building!)

JACHIN AND BOAZ

The two pillars that stood at the entrance to the Temple had names! One was called Jachin and the other Boaz. These words mean "sustainer" and "aggressive protector." They describe the Lord's relationship with Israel.

THE BRAZEN SEA

You won't find this sea on a map! The brazen sea was a huge bowl filled with water. The priests washed here. The sea held 10,000 to 15,000 gallons of water—about as much as a big backyard swimming pool.

THE ALTAR

The priests offered daily sacrifices here as they prayed to God. The altar stood 15 feet tall.

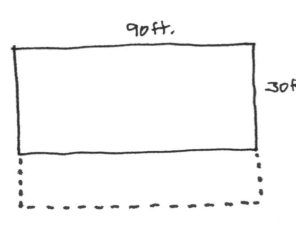

90 ft.

30 ft.

SMALL PACKAGES

Solomon's Temple was about as long as a basketball court but narrower. It wasn't a meeting place, so it didn't need to be big. When the people came for a special festival, they gathered outside in the large courtyard.

MAKING MEMORIES

Solomon's Temple was built on the same mountain where Abraham went to sacrifice Isaac.

ANOTHER ARK

The Ark of the Covenant was different than Noah's ark. It was a beautiful chest that held the stone tablets on which God had written the Ten Commandments. The Ark rested beneath two carved, winged figures known as cherubim. When the Temple was destroyed in 586 B.C., the Ark of the Covenant disappeared. Some people think it may still be hidden in Jerusalem or elsewhere.

A SCARY ASSIGNMENT

The Holy of Holies was so sacred that only one person—the high priest—could enter it once a year. There he made a sacrifice for the sins of the whole nation. The high priest took his job seriously. Entering the Holy of Holies with the wrong attitude might mean his death. He even wore bells that jingled as he walked so the people knew that he was still alive.

MANY HANDS MAKE LIGHT WORK

Solomon's beautiful Temple took just seven years to build. Princes, priests, the rich, and the poor all pitched in and worked together.

ROYAL LIMERICKS

AFTER THE TIME OF THE JUDGES, the Israelites asked God to let them have kings like the other nations. The king's success depended on his allegiance to God. Some of the kings were good, but many of them were not. They allowed the people to worship foreign gods and even worshiped them themselves! Here are some amazing facts about the kings of Israel and Judah.

YOUNGEST KING—JOASH

(2 Chronicles 24:1)

Joash was the youngest king's name.

At seven he started his reign.

Then he listened to men

Who led him to sin,

And his reign was never the same.

SHORTEST REIGN—ZIMRI (1 Kings 16)

King Zimri ruled just seven days,

Before setting his palace ablaze.

He feared that his rival

Would cut short his survival

So he took his own life anyways.

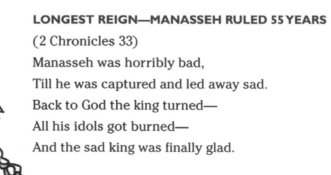

LONGEST REIGN—MANASSEH RULED 55 YEARS

(2 Chronicles 33)

Manasseh was horribly bad,

Till he was captured and led away sad.

Back to God the king turned—

All his idols got burned—

And the sad king was finally glad.

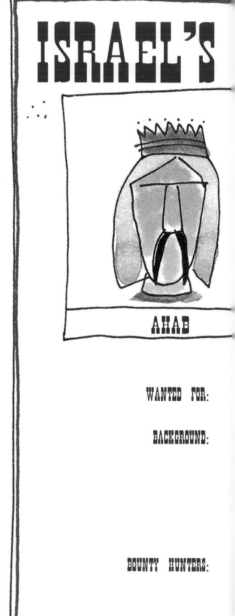

ISRAEL'S

AHAB

WANTED FOR:

BACKGROUND:

BOUNTY HUNTERS:

WISEST—SOLOMON

(1 Kings 3)

There once was a good king named Sol
Who asked for the best gift of all.
He prayed to be wise
So God answered his cries
And gave him riches as well.

Q: How many songs and proverbs did Solomon write?
A: 1005 songs and 3000 proverbs (1 King 4:29-32).
Look in the book of Proverbs to find some of his wise sayings.

MOST WANTED

JEZEBEL

BEST KING—JOSIAH (2 Kings 22–23)

The book with God's words had been lost
And the people had suffered the cost.
But Josiah retrieved it,
The people believed it,
And idols at all cost were tossed!

Turning people away from the living God.

King Ahab married a woman from another country. He let her lead people to serve the idols her people worshiped. Because King Ahab let Queen Jezebel do this, he made God angrier than any other king of Israel (1 Kings 16:33).

Must be able to call down fire from heaven to set a sacrifice doused with water on fire in front of 450 idol-worshipers (Turn to the story of Elijah, and you'll see what happened.)

ELIJAH AND ELISHA

1 Kings 17–19

ELIJAH AND ELISHA WERE GREAT PROPHETS who lived around 850 B.C. in the land of Israel. Elijah was like a dad to Elisha. Right before Elijah was taken up to heaven in a whirlwind, he asked Elisha if there was anything he wanted. Elisha asked for twice as much of the spirit God had given Elijah. Remember, a double portion was the size of the blessing that the firstborn son received, and Elisha was Elijah's son in the faith.

Sometimes it's hard to keep these two guys straight. Not only are their names so close, but some of their miracles are also alike!

CHARIOTS OF FIRE

Q.What two men in the Bible never died?

A. Elijah—He was taken up to heaven in a chariot with horses of fire.

   Enoch—The Bible says "Enoch walked with God, and he was not, for God took him." What a way to go!

ELIJAH

Elijah told a widow that if she made some bread for him out of the handful of flour that she had left, God would supply her for the rest of the famine. He did!

Later, the widow's son died and was brought back to life by Elijah.

In a contest on Mount Carmel, the sacrifice offered by the 450 false prophets would not burn. But Elijah prayed and fire from heaven came and took his offering.

Elijah ran for his life from the evil queen, Jezebel. When he was alone and afraid, God spoke to him in a "still small voice."

When King Ahaziah sent 102 soldiers to arrest Elijah, he called down fire from heaven. The fire killed them.

Elijah took off his outer cloak and struck the waters of the Jordan River with it. Miraculously the river dried up.

ELISHA

 Elisha's first miracle was just like Elijah's. He took off his cloak and struck the waters of the river, and they opened for him.

 When the city water supply of Jericho turned bad, Elisha threw a bowl of salt into the pool, and the Lord made it safe to drink again.

 Like Elijah, Elisha also helped a poor widow. She had only one jar of oil, essential for cooking. Elisha had her collect all the empty jars her friends would lend her. God miraculously filled them all from her original jar.

 A wealthy woman let Elisha stay at her house. Years later her son became ill and died. Elisha raised him back to life.

 While preparing food for the sons of the prophets, the cook accidently put poisoned gourds in the pot. Elisha threw meal in the pot, and the food was fine.

 The Lord multiplied Elisha's 20 barley loaves and few heads of grain to feed 100 men.

 Elisha told Naaman, the leper, to dip seven times in the Jordan River. Naaman thought it was a crazy command—but he reluctantly obeyed and was healed.

 A man accidently threw a borrowed ax into the water. Elisha tossed a stick in after it and the heavy metal ax-head floated to the surface!

 The King of Syria sent his army to surround Elisha's city and capture him. Elisha prayed. God sent an army of angels in chariots of fire.

 Elisha told King Joash to take some arrows and strike the ground. Joash struck only three times, so that was the number of victories he had against the Syrians. Imagine if he had struck 100 times?

 After Elisha died some men put another body in Elisha's tomb. It touched his bones. The minute it did, the man came back to life. Whoa!

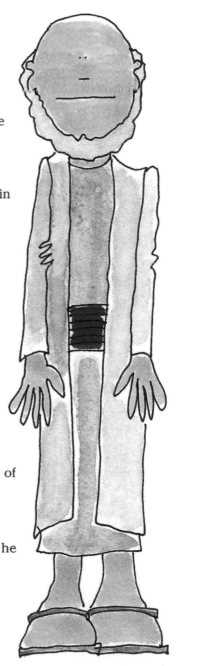

JONAH

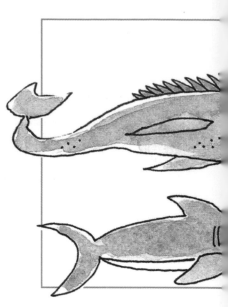

God's prophets usually spoke only to the people of Israel, but one time God told Jonah to go to the city of Nineveh. Nineveh was the capital of Assyria, a ruthless, bloodthirsty empire that was always breathing down Israel's neck. You can see why Jonah really didn't want to go there. When Jonah heard that God would destroy Nineveh if the people didn't repent, he said, "Great! If I don't preach, they won't repent and—poof—they'll be history." But just like today, God loved the people in Nineveh and wanted to save them.

STOP THAT MAN!

Jonah tried to run away from God. He went to Joppa and bought a one-way ticket for Tarshish. But soon after his vacation cruise began, a storm hit. He was thrown overboard and then swallowed and thrown up by a big fish. After that he decided maybe he should go preach to Nineveh after all.

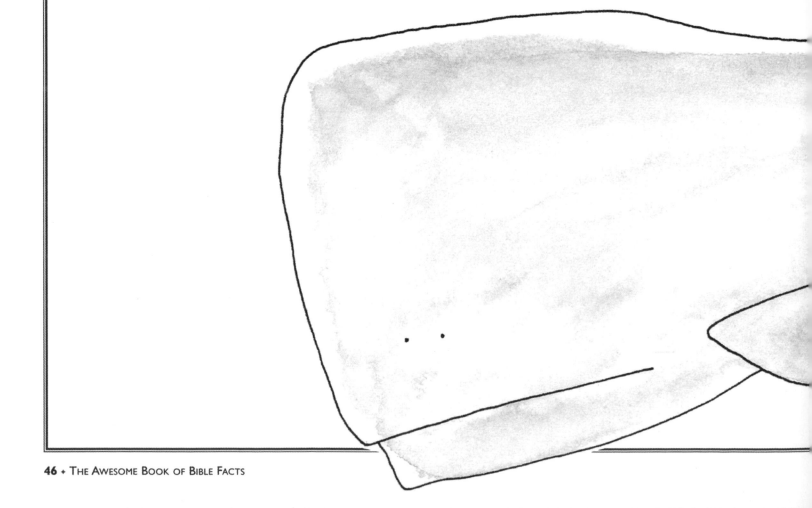

A MIRACLE FISH

What kind of a "fish" swallowed Jonah? No one knows exactly. Many people speculate that it was a great white shark. A 19-foot shark can swallow a man whole. Large sperm whales have also been known to visit the Mediterranean. Sperm whales grow up to 65 feet long—plenty of room in there. Or it might just have been a big fish! Whatever it was, the Bible says God provided it especially to rescue Jonah.

THE WINNER IS . . .

At the storm's worst—when the ship looked doomed—the sailors cast lots to figure out who had caused all the trouble. The lots pointed to Jonah. Casting lots often meant tossing two flat stones on a table. They were painted black on one side and white on the other. If the rocks landed two whites up, the answer was yes; two blacks, the answer was no. One of each meant "wait."

SEE FOR YOURSELF

The big fish wasn't the only interesting thing God sent Jonah's way. Read the whole story in the book of Jonah and try to find these four other things: a storm, a plant, a worm, and the east wind.*

FOR REAL

Did Jonah really exist? Some people think this story is just a legend (it *is* pretty incredible!). But Jonah was a real person. In 2 Kings 14:25, he is mentioned as a prophet during the reign of Jeroboam II of Israel. Jesus also spoke of Jonah in Matthew 12.

*Hint: Chapter 1 (verse 4) and chapter 4 (verses 6, 7, and 8).

DANIEL

Daniel 1–6

DANIEL AND HIS FRIENDS Hananiah, Mishael, and Azariah were captured by the Babylonians and taken from Israel about 605 B.C. As young leaders of the upper class of Israel, they were given three years of college education—only they didn't get to choose their subjects! They learned Chaldean (the Babylonian language) and studied literature. Then they were made part of the king's court and given important positions.

POPULARITY BREEDS CONTEMPT

Daniel, now called Belteshazzar, and his friends Shadrach, Meshach, and Abednego (names given to them by the Babylonians) became popular with the king. Other officials grew jealous. They reported Daniel's three friends for refusing to bow to King Nebuchadnezzar's golden image. The king ordered them thrown into a huge, fiery furnace. The furnace was usually used to melt metal, so it was hot, hot, hot. And then the king ordered it to be heated seven times as hot as usual!

MELTING POINTS

- Iron: 1535° C
- Gold: 1064° C
- Silver: 961° C
- Bronze: 630° C
- Toast: toasts at 93° C!

EAT YOUR VEGETABLES

When they first arrived in Babylon, Daniel and his friends wouldn't eat the king's food because it had been offered to idols. Instead, they asked for plain vegetables. After ten days, they looked healthier than the Babylonian guys eating the king's rich food!

HUNGER PAINS

Q. How do you know Daniel's rescue was a miracle?
A. Because Daniel's accusers were dropped into the den, and the lions ate them before they hit bottom!

NO SURPRISE

Shadrach, Meshach, and Abednego knew all about the fiery furnace. This wasn't the first time the Babylonians had put someone on the hot seat. But nothing would change the young men's minds. What a surprise for the king when he saw *four* men in the flames—and the fourth one looked like the Son of God!

WHERE WAS DANIEL?

Where was Daniel all this time? Some people think he was out of the city on government business, and that his absence gave the officials a chance to move against his friends.

YOU'RE NEXT!

Daniel got his chance to trust God many years later. He was accused of praying to God instead of the new Persian king, Darius. The Persians preferred the lion's den to the Babylonians' hot old furnace. Usually a prisoner would be thrown in and devoured immediately. Imagine the surprise when Daniel walked out unharmed the next day!

ESTHER

Esther 1–9

ESTHER WAS A JEWISH WOMAN who, like Joseph and Daniel, played a part in saving her people. She lived in the country of Persia. It happened that King Ahasuerus (his Persian name was Xerxes) was looking for a new queen. Esther won the job. At the same time, Esther's Uncle Mordecai found himself in hot water because he wouldn't bow to anyone but the living God. He wouldn't even bow to Haman, the king's right-hand man. So Haman wanted to kill *all* the Jews. He talked the king into signing a paper that gave him permission. But God used Mordecai and Esther to rescue the Jewish people.

EVERYDAY MIRACLES

Even though God isn't mentioned by name, lots of miracles take place. The book of Esther reads much like our lives. It's full of "just happens". . . that just happen to be God at work!

• The king just happens to welcome Esther into his presence (coming unannounced could have resulted in her execution).

• Because Haman announces the date he plans to kill the Jews, Mordecai and Esther just happen to have time to stop the slaughter of their people.

• The king just happens to be restless one night and ask that the royal records be read to him. (He hears that Mordecai discovered a plot and saved the king's life.)

• Haman just happens to build a gallows to hang Mordecai. But when the king finds out how bad he is, and how loyal Mordecai is, Haman just happens to be the one hanged!

THE ROYAL HOUSEKEEPING SEAL OF APPROVAL

King Ahasuerus loved Esther so much that he promised her up to half his kingdom. But he couldn't cancel his decree to destroy the Jews. Changing a royal order was impossible once the king's seal (usually his signet ring pressed in wax) was applied.

EXPRESS MAIL

The king couldn't change his order, but he did the next best thing. He sent his finest horsemen to all 126 provinces with new orders that the Jewish people could fight back! The messengers beat the deadline, but they wouldn't have had to run nearly so fast if the king had owned a fax machine!

SOMETIMES YOU WIN, SOMETIMES YOU LOSE

King Ahasuerus ruled from 486-465 B.C. He is most remembered for losing a big battle against Greece. This might have taken place between chapters 1 and 2 of the book of Esther.

AN ESTHER LAUDER BEAUTY MAKEOVER

To win the position of queen, Esther first spent six months softening her skin with oil made from myrrh. Then she spent six *more* months using perfumes and other beauty treatments. All of this before she even saw the king!

BIBLE-TIME MAKEUP

Eye shadow: green from powdered turquoise or malachite stones
Eyeliner: black from kohl
Lip gloss: red from the ocher plant
Hand cream: red from the henna plant mixed with oil and applied to the palms of the hands, soles of feet, and hair.
Perfume: spices or flowers mixed with oil

Official Decree from King A

to the satraps, governors over each province the princes of each people.

Let it be decreed on this day of the month

the king will pay ten thousand talents of silve

hands of those who carry on the Kin

siness, to put into the Ki

is decree

The

NEHEMIAH

Nehemiah 1–8

Jerusalem, God's special city, had been through many battles. In one of the worst, the city was burned and its walls turned to rubble by an army from Babylon. Years later—about 500 years before Christ—the Babylonians were beaten by the Persians, and thousands of Jews were taken to Persia (that's where Esther's adventures took place). Many Jews, like Nehemiah, held important positions in Persian society. One day a messenger from Judah talked to Nehemiah. He told Nehemiah that the walls of Jerusalem had never been repaired. The people were discouraged. When Nehemiah heard this, he asked the king for a leave of absence. He wanted to go to Jerusalem and rebuild the walls of the City of God.

THE ROYAL CUPBEARER

As the cupbearer to the king, part of Nehemiah's job was tasting the king's wine. He made sure it wasn't poisoned. King Artaxerxes was extra-sensitive to this because his father had been assassinated.

AN UNUSUAL WORK PARTY

Girls never worked with men in those days. But this was such an important project that one man named Shallum let his daughters help.

A LONG VACATION

Asking the king for time off was risky business. Nehemiah could have lost his life if the king had been angry. But the king sent him off with letters for safe passage, an armed guard, and even requests for lumber from Asaph, the keeper of the king's forest.

BIG BREACHES

The walls of a city were its chief line of defense. They were often 50 feet high. If there was a hole or breach in the wall, enemy soldiers could get inside, open the main gates for the rest of the army, and capture the city.

STICKS AND STONES . . .

Have you ever been laughed at? Two wicked men from neighboring lands, Sanballat and Tobiah, made fun of the Jews. They mocked them for trying to rebuild the walls out of the rubble. Do you know what Nehemiah did? He prayed, and God answered his prayer.

COME ONE, COME ALL

The families in Jerusalem each worked on a separate part of the wall. They replaced the stones, built new doors, and made new hinges and locks. Part of Nehemiah's wall has been found. It is eight feet thick in some places.

A HAPPY END

The wall was finished in just 52 days. Afterward, Ezra the scribe read to the people from God's Word. They were sorry they hadn't obeyed God sooner. They began to cry. But Nehemiah said to them, "Do not cry, for the joy of the Lord is your strength." So the people had a great celebration.

EN GUARDE!

When Sanballat and Tobiah saw that their mocking wasn't stopping the people from rebuilding the wall, they became angry. Nehemiah knew that they might attack the city before the walls were finished. So he ordered the people to carry weapons and tools at the same time. They even slept in their work clothes! That way they were always ready to work or fight.

FEASTS AND FESTS

GOD LOVES IT when people get together to worship Him and remember what He has done for them. Because He is a God of celebration, He set aside special festivals for the Jewish people. These were celebrated every year.

PASSOVER AND THE FEAST OF UNLEAVENED BREAD

The most important festival of the year for Jewish people was, and still is, Passover. This festival marks the time God delivered His people from Egypt. The tenth and final plague was to be the death of the firstborn in every household in Egypt. But God warned the Jewish people to sacrifice a lamb, wiping some of its blood on their doorposts. When the angel of the Lord saw the blood, he "passed over" that house and the firstborn didn't die. Jesus, the Lamb of God, was crucified during the Passover celebration.

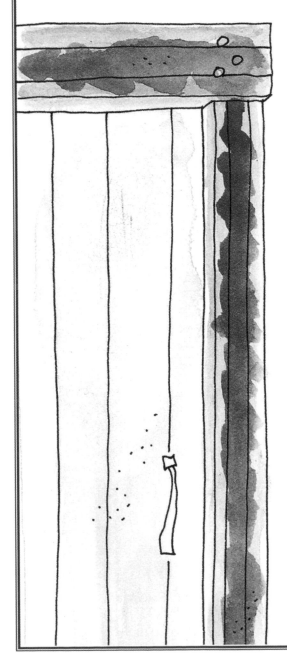

FESTIVAL OF TABERNACLES OR FEAST OF BOOTHS

At the end of September the people held a feast to commemorate the journey in the wilderness. In the wilderness, the Jews had lived in tents or "tabernacles." During this festival all the people built booths of branches and leaves and lived in them for a week in Jerusalem. Four large candelabra gave light to the whole city from the Temple during this feast. This may have been when Jesus stood up and said, "I am the light of the world" (John 7:37).

PENTECOST OR THE FESTIVAL OF WEEKS

Pentecost means "50 days" in Greek. This festival was held 50 days (seven weeks) after Passover and celebrated the spring harvest. During the wheat harvest and after the barley harvest, two large loaves of bread were baked from the fresh grain and offered to the Lord. Pentecost also commemorated the giving of the Ten Commandments at Mount Sinai—because it took the Israelites 50 days to reach the mountain after leaving Egypt.

IT GETS YOUR GOAT

The Day of Atonement was the day the high priest would go before God on behalf of the people. Early in the morning he would kill one goat for a sacrifice. Then the high priest laid his hand on a second goat's head, symbolically laying the sins of the people onto that animal. He sent it away into the wilderness forever. This is where the word "scapegoat" comes from. That's why people who get blamed for things they didn't do are called "scapegoats" today.

HANUKKAH

The Festival of Lights or Hanukkah is a more recent celebration that's not mentioned in the Bible. It occurs in December. During a time of struggle against Syria, a brave Jewish leader named Judas Maccabeus led an army that drove the Syrians out of the land. Then he cleansed the Temple, which the Syrians had spoiled. Legend says that when the Jews entered the Temple there was only one day's supply of oil for the lamp. But God miraculously kept the lamps burning for eight days. So this festival lasts for eight days. Jewish boys and girls often get a gift on each of those days.

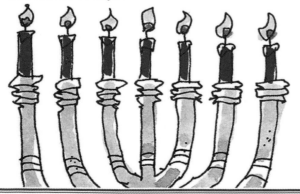

SAYINGS FROM THE BIBLE

A LOT OF FAMILIAR PHRASES we use today are taken from the Bible. Some are from the Old Testament, and some are from the New Testament. Do you recognize any of these? Note: If you look these up, you will need to use a King James version of the Bible to find the exact words.

THE APPLE OF MY EYE

God calls the children of Israel the apple of His eye in Deuteronomy 32:10. In case you're wondering, the "apple" of the eye is the pupil. God takes care of His people just like you take care of your eyes!

AN EYE FOR AN EYE

An eye for an eye means paying someone back for something they did to you in the same measure (Exodus 21:24). But Jesus said, "If someone slaps you on one cheek, let him slap the other one, too."

SPARE THE ROD AND SPOIL THE CHILD

Spare the rod and spoil the child is taken from Proverbs 13:24. Parents are to discipline their children, so they grow up knowing right from wrong.

THE HANDWRITING ON THE WALL

When people say they see the "handwriting on the wall," it means they see trouble ahead. In the book of Daniel, King Belshazzar saw mysterious writing suddenly appear on his palace wall. Daniel interpreted the writing, which told of the king's downfall.

Handwriting on the wall

A WOLF IN SHEEP'S CLOTHING

Jesus told His disciples to beware of false prophets who dress in sheep's clothing but inwardly are like hungry wolves. They look kind and good on the outside, but underneath they are leading people away from God.

THE POWERS THAT BE

The powers that be refers to someone in authority: "We'll have to ask the powers that be and get their approval." This is taken from Romans 13:1, "For there is no power but of God, the powers that be are ordained of God."

THE SKIN OF YOUR TEETH

When someone escapes by "the skin of his teeth," he's made a very narrow escape indeed. That's what happened to Job in Job 19:20.

A DROP IN THE BUCKET

A tiny amount compared to something larger, as in: "A hundred dollars is just a drop in the bucket for that millionaire!" This comes from Isaiah 40:15, where all the nations of the world are considered a drop in the bucket compared to the awesome God of the universe.

The Birth of Jesus

Matthew 2; Luke 2

VACATIONS ARE SUPPOSED TO BE FUN, but Mary and Joseph's trip to Bethlehem would have been very "taxing." Hey, that's what the trip was for—Mary and Joseph were there to be put on the Roman tax rolls! The journey was long and hard for a pregnant woman, and especially for a couple who had already endured the looks and whispers of their neighbors over Mary's mysterious pregnancy. Who was this child inside her? What did it all mean?

SLOW GOING

Both Mary and Joseph probably walked the 80 miles from Nazareth to Bethlehem. It would have taken them five days or longer, since Mary was nine months pregnant. Today, you could make this trip in less than two hours by car.

ROOM FOR TWO, PLEASE

The inn that Mary and Joseph were turned away from was most likely an upstairs room of someone's house—maybe even one of Joseph's relatives. The word Luke uses for "inn" is the same Greek word he uses for the "upper room" where the disciples shared the Last Supper with Jesus.

WAY AWAY IN A MANGER

In Jesus' time, people sometimes kept farm animals in a cave near the village rather than in a wooden barn like today. The manger was really a feeding trough where the larger animals ate hay and grains. Sometimes a newborn lamb would be placed in the manger to keep it warm. Jesus, the Lamb of God, slept there, too.

WISE GUYS

How many wise men were there? Most people think three, but only because three gifts are mentioned. They came from the East (perhaps from Persia) and were priest-advisers to the their king. Some people think there were dozens of wise men, who showed up in all their splendor accompanied by armed guards. They think this because the wise men were so impressive that Herod and all of Jerusalem were alarmed by their presence. However, the wise men assured Herod they weren't there to start trouble—only to see "him who was born king of the Jews."

STRANGE BABY GIFTS

The gifts brought by the wise men were fancy gifts to bring to a poor newborn. *Gold* was a sign of royalty. *Frankincense*, used to make incense for the Temple, came from the gummy resin of a tree grown in Arabia. People gathered the resin from cuts made in the tree bark—like tapping trees for maple syrup. *Myrrh* was a perfume that scented the holy anointing oil.

These three valuable gifts may have been sold or traded to pay for the poor family's emergency trip to Egypt to escape King Herod.

CITY ON A HILL

IN JESUS' DAY, Jerusalem was a bustling metropolitan city built on the tops of five hills. But the first time Jerusalem is mentioned in the Bible is before Israel is even a nation—in Genesis, when Abram meets with the king of Salem (short for Jerusalem). The Canaanites ruled Jerusalem (or Jebus, as they called it) until the Israelites won it during their conquest of the Promised Land. From the time David took the Ark of the Covenant there to stay, Jerusalem was set apart as the City of God. It is the most famous city in the Bible.

HEROD'S PALACE

King Herod's palace was built like a fortress (Herod wasn't well-liked). Pilate sent Jesus to Herod on the night of His arrest.

CALVARY (GOLGOTHA)

No one is sure exactly where Jesus died. Many people think it was on a hill in this area.

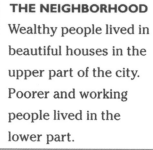

THE NEIGHBORHOOD

Wealthy people lived in beautiful houses in the upper part of the city. Poorer and working people lived in the lower part.

AMPHITHEATER

King Herod introduced Greek and Roman culture to Jerusalem by building an outdoor theater where plays were performed and speeches given.

URBAN SPRAWL

Jerusalem grew a lot from the time of David to the time of Jesus. The part of the large map colored pink is the earlier Jerusalem, where David had his capital. In those days, the city was shaped like a giant footprint. It was so small that it would fit inside the Louisiana Superdome—with room to spare!

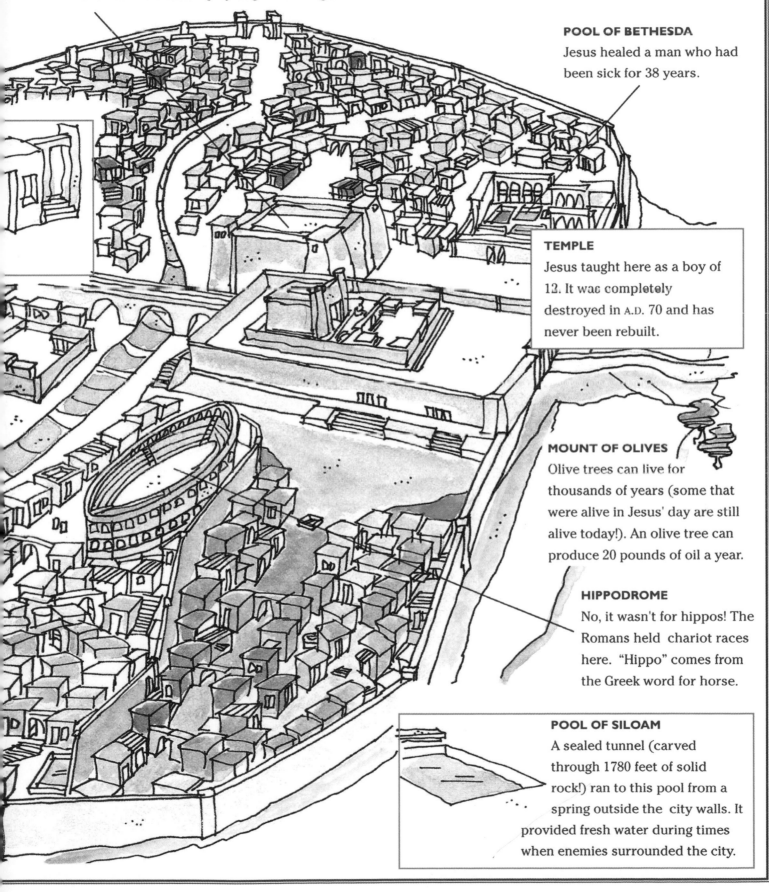

FORTRESS OF ANTONIA

Pontius Pilate and hundreds of Roman soldiers lived here to protect the Temple. You can still see etchings on the stone floor where soldiers played games and gambled. Jesus stood here when His death sentence was announced.

POOL OF BETHESDA

Jesus healed a man who had been sick for 38 years.

TEMPLE

Jesus taught here as a boy of 12. It was completely destroyed in A.D. 70 and has never been rebuilt.

MOUNT OF OLIVES

Olive trees can live for thousands of years (some that were alive in Jesus' day are still alive today!). An olive tree can produce 20 pounds of oil a year.

HIPPODROME

No, it wasn't for hippos! The Romans held chariot races here. "Hippo" comes from the Greek word for horse.

POOL OF SILOAM

A sealed tunnel (carved through 1780 feet of solid rock!) ran to this pool from a spring outside the city walls. It provided fresh water during times when enemies surrounded the city.

BY THE BEAUTIFUL SEA

Capernaum •

AFTER JOHN THE BAPTIST HAD BEEN ARRESTED, Jesus moved from Nazareth to a city called Capernaum. Jesus moved because the people in Nazareth didn't believe in Him. In fact they tried to throw Him off a cliff! Capernaum was on the shore of the Sea of Galilee (it wasn't really a sea; it was a lake about 13 miles long). Here Jesus began calling His disciples, the fishermen Peter, Andrew, James, and John. Fishing was great in the Sea of Galilee. Matthew, the tax collector, was also from Capernaum. He may have been collecting taxes on all of the fish caught!

MIRACLE CITY

Jesus did at least 18 miracles along the shores of the Sea of Galilee. Ten of them were done in Capernaum, including the time Jesus healed the paralyzed man who was lowered through the roof by his four good friends.

INSTANT TROUBLE

Because of its location on an earthquake fault line, its low altitude (690 feet below sea level), and the high hills that rise from it on either side, violent storms often brew without warning on the Sea of Galilee. The mountains act like an "air funnel," driving high winds down their slopes and onto the water. The disciples got caught in two of these storms.

CATCH OF THE DAY

Jesus and Peter had to pay taxes but didn't have any money. So Jesus told Peter to cast a hook into the water. Peter caught a fish— probably a *tilapia* fish. This fish usually keeps its babies in its mouth. But when the mom needs a break, she picks up a shiny object. She holds it in her mouth as a gate to keep the babies out. The fish that Peter caught had picked up a coin— just the right coin to pay their Temple tax.

THE CENTURION'S GIFT

A Roman centurion stationed in Capernaum built a synagogue for the Jews. A synagogue was a place Jewish people met when they weren't near the Temple.

MEET YOU AT THE SPA

There were hot springs on the western shore of the lake. If you were hurting, you went there hoping the swirling warm water would ease your pain (like a big hot tub). Jesus healed many people along these shores.

WORLD'S GREATEST SERMON

One day, Jesus went up onto the slope of a hill in Galilee and preached the most famous sermon in the world, the Sermon on the Mount. You can read all about it starting in Matthew 5. Matthew is the first book in the New Testament and was written by—you guessed it—the tax collector from Capernaum!

IT'S A MIRACLE!

A MIRACLE IS SOMETHING THAT A PERSON can't do on his own. It's not magic because there is no sleight-of-hand or trickery. It's real. Jesus performed many great miracles in front of thousands of people. The Bible records 33 of them. But the apostle John tells us that if everything that Jesus did were written down, "even the world itself could not contain the books"! The Bible uses some interesting words to describe miracles. They are called "wonders" because they astonished the people who watched them happen. They are called "signs" because they showed people that Jesus was different—He was God's Son. And they are called "powers" because they proved that Jesus had power over the world.

UNCLEAN!

In Bible times, leprosy was a terrible disease. It caused numbness and deformity and skin problems. Lepers weren't allowed to touch anyone. They had to live outside the city. And whenever anyone passed by, they had to cry out, "Unclean! Unclean!" so that everyone would know they had this disease.

IS THERE A DOCTOR IN THE HOUSE?

Jewish writings tell us that physicians were common in Israel. Doctors had to get a special license to practice from city authorities. The writer of the gospel of Luke was a physician. Luke uses more medical words than the other gospel writers.

NINE THINGS JESUS HEALED

1. blindness
2. paralysis
3. curvature of the spine
4. a severed ear
5. epilepsy
6. bleeding
7. insanity
8. leprosy
9. dropsy (a heart or kidney condition that causes swelling)

SABBATH MIRACLES

Jesus was always trying to get the religious leaders to see the things that were really important in life. The Pharisees had made a rule that no one could be healed on the Sabbath. But that wasn't God's rule. So Jesus healed people on the Sabbath to show them how far wrong they'd gone.

Q: How many people did Jesus heal on the Sabbath?
A: Seven—two women and five men.

WATER WONDERS

Jesus...

1. walked on water
2. calmed the storm with His word

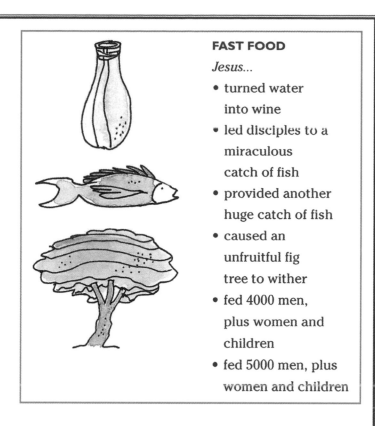

FAST FOOD

Jesus...

- turned water into wine
- led disciples to a miraculous catch of fish
- provided another huge catch of fish
- caused an unfruitful fig tree to wither
- fed 4000 men, plus women and children
- fed 5000 men, plus women and children

FISH FRY

The little boy who supplied the fish and bread with which Jesus fed the hungry crowd had brought five loaves (flat biscuits) of bread and two fish. There were 5000 men with women and children besides—perhaps 10,000 people in all. Even if each person ate only half of what the boy brought for himself, Jesus miraculously provided 25,000 loaves of bread and 10,000 fish!

Five thousand three hundred Eighty two...

SARDINES, ANYONE?

The fish that Jesus multiplied were likely a type of lake sardine called *belak*, a small fish that was eaten dried and salted. Salted fish were popular in Jesus' day. There was a big fish market at the Fish Gate in Jerusalem.

STORIES JESUS TOLD

Matthew 13; Luke 15

JESUS TOLD HIS DISCIPLES many parables—about 30 are recorded in the Bible. A parable is a story. In His stories, Jesus talked about farming and money and things that everyday people could understand. But His parables were more than just stories. They were stories that taught a lesson. Jesus used these parables to teach the disciples many things about Himself. He also used stories to hide things from those people who had hardened their hearts against Him.

THE PEARL OF GREAT PRICE

Jesus said, "The kingdom of heaven is like a merchant who was looking for a valuable pearl. When he found the perfect pearl, he sold everything he had and bought it."

IT'S A NATURAL

Among all of the great gems—diamonds, rubies, sapphires, emeralds—the pearl is the only one made by a living creature. It is also the only one that comes from the sea.

MINT CONDITION

Coins were invented about 600 years before Christ in Lydia, a country in what is now Turkey. Before that, gold and other precious metals were weighed on a scale.

LIGHTEN UP!

The women who were listening to Jesus would have enjoyed this parable. They were the ones who made bread for their families. "Leaven" was the ingredient that made bread soft instead of hard. In Bible times the leaven was a small piece of dough that had turned sour. The women added that to the new batch—the same way sourdough bread is made today.

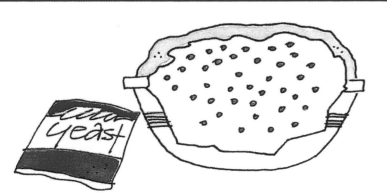

SPREADING THE GOOD NEWS

Jesus said, "The kingdom of heaven is like the leaven that a woman mixes into the flour so that it will rise." That means that when one person tells another person about God and His ways, and that person tells another—pretty soon everybody knows.

POCKET CHANGE

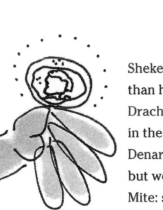

Shekel: A silver or gold coin that weighed less than half an ounce.

Drachma: This is the Roman coin that the woman in the parable lost. Equal to a denarius.

Denarius: a Roman coin about the size of a dime but worth a day's wages.

Mite: smallest coin. Two of them made one cent.

Talent: 3000 shekels (about 75 pounds of precious metal).

THE LOST COIN

Jesus said, "If a woman had ten coins and lost one, wouldn't she turn on all of the lights and search every nook and cranny of the house until she found it? And when she found it, wouldn't she call all her friends so they could share her joy? So all of the angels in heaven rejoice over one sinner who turns away from his sins."

INTERESTING PEOPLE JESUS KNEW

A s JESUS JOURNEYED THROUGH ISRAEL, he met rabbis and Roman soldiers, righteous people and sinners, adults and children. We're told of only a few in particular. But these give us insight into the very different kinds of people Jesus touched.

ZACCHEUS

Zaccheus was short, rich, and unpopular. His name means "pure" or "righteous one" but somewhere he went wrong. While living in Jericho he worked (or probably bribed someone) to become the chief tax collector.

In those days a tax collector could charge much more than the actual tax as long as he gave a certain amount to the Roman government. Zaccheus got rich cheating

people. Not a great way to make friends! So when Jesus walked through town, nobody made room for him. He had to climb a sycamore tree—a fig tree—to see Jesus. He was probably embarrassed when Jesus called his name. But soon Zaccheus' whole life changed. He told Jesus, "I will repay anyone I've cheated four times as much as I took." That was twice what the Jewish law required.

JAIRUS' DAUGHTER

Jesus' friendships give us a perfect picture of how God looks at us. Jesus didn't care if a person was poor or rich, popular or unpopular, weak or strong. One day Jairus, the leader of the Jewish synagogue, came to ask Jesus to heal his daughter. On the way, a poor, sick woman reached out and touched Jesus' clothing, hoping to be healed. Jairus was a leader—we don't even know the woman's name. Jairus had money—he could even afford professional mourners for his daughter. The woman had nothing. But Jesus helped them both.

THE CENTURION FROM CAPERNAUM

While Jesus was teaching in the seaside village of Capernaum, a centurion sent to him and asked if Jesus would heal his servant. A centurion was a Roman military officer. He commanded 100 men (like the number of years in a century). This centurion believed that Jesus could heal his servant with just a word. That's more than the Jewish leaders believed! The centurion was in charge of people, and they did what he told them. And he was under higher authorities, so he had learned to do what he was told. He knew that Jesus had the same kind of authority over sickness. If He ordered it to go, it would go.

WAYS JESUS HEALED

- rubbed mud in a man's eyes
- touched the leper
- lifted a woman by the hand
- honored the faith of friends
- called Lazarus out of the tomb
- spoke a word
- let the hem of His robe be touched
- raised a widow's son

THE WOMAN AT THE WELL

While passing through Samaria, Jesus stopped to talk to a woman getting water from a well. The disciples were amazed. Jewish teachers never talked to a woman in public. And Jews looked down on the Samaritans because they were people of Jewish heritage who had mixed with the Assyrians. To top it off, this woman had been married five times and was now with a man who was not her husband! She probably came to the well at noon to avoid the gossip of other women, who usually came to draw water in the cool of the morning. But Jesus didn't ridicule her. He saw a person created by God who was hurting. Jesus gave her hope.

HOSANNAH!

Luke 19

HURRY! HE'S COMING! THE MESSIAH'S HERE! The children were shouting to each other. Word had traveled fast that Jesus was coming to Jerusalem. And during Passover. "This must be the time when Jesus will get rid of the Romans and start His perfect government," people thought. He had already miraculously fed thousands of their friends. They thought the Messiah was now going to use His power to become an earthly king and save them from the Romans.

THE CROWDS GO WILD

The people shouted "Hosannah!" The word means "Save now!" That's what they expected Jesus to do. Hosannah was a joyful shout that came from Psalm 118:25.

LET'S HAVE A PARADE

As Jesus rode into Jerusalem, the people were cheering, waving palm branches, and laying their cloaks on the ground as a carpet for Him. This is how people welcomed a king in those days. It was like a ticker-tape parade.

MESSIAH

Messiah means "anointed one"—someone who has been set apart for a special task. The Old Testament had promised that God would send an anointed One to save them. Earthly kings were anointed for their work when sweet-smelling olive oil was poured on their heads.

DANGER AHEAD

Before Jesus entered the city on Sunday, He began to cry. He knew the people would turn away from Him in just a few days. By Friday they had laid aside their palm branches and were shouting, "Crucify Him!"

WHERE'S THE COCONUT?

Oops. The palm trees in Israel were date palms, not coconut palms. Date palms grow about 90 feet tall and have branches nine feet long. They provided roofing material (branches), camel feed (seeds), rope (from the crowns), and fruit.

FIT FOR A KING

In wartime, a conquering king would ride into his new city on a big, powerful horse. But if he came in peace, he rode a donkey. Jesus rode a donkey, just as prophets had foretold 400 years earlier (Zechariah 9:9).

THE LAST SUPPER

Luke 22; John 13

ON THE NIGHT WHEN JESUS WAS BETRAYED, He had the disciples arrange for a special Passover meal. It was early for Passover, but this "last supper" was the final time Jesus would be with His friends before His crucifixion. He sent them into Jerusalem to find a man carrying a water pitcher. Jesus knew that man would lead them to the place where they could celebrate the meal together. Jesus had many good things to teach the disciples through the symbols of the meal.

MORE PILLOWS, PLEASE

The disciples didn't sit at a table the way we normally do. They lay down on the floor, propped up on one elbow. Passover was usually celebrated this way because in ancient times this is how people who weren't slaves ate their meals. It reminded the people that God had set them free.

FOUR SPECIAL CUPS

Four cups of wine were used in the Passover meal. When Jesus said, "This cup is the new covenant in my blood which is poured out for you," He would have been raising the cup that symbolized redemption. Jesus "redeemed" us by paying the price for our sins on the cross.

HIDE AND SEEK

During the meal, three pieces of unleavened bread were kept in a special container. Two pieces of bread were eaten, but one was kept separate until the end of the meal. When Jesus broke the bread and said, "This is my body," He was telling the disciples that He was going to be separated from the Father and Holy Spirit. He would be broken and brought back to life.

THE GREATEST OF ALL

After supper, Jesus wrapped Himself in a towel and washed the disciples' feet. This job was usually done by the lowest servant. Now it was being done by the God of creation! Jesus want to teach His disciples to always serve one another.

THE MAN WITH A PITCHER

Finding the man carrying a pitcher of water would have been easy. Carrying water was a woman's job, so a man with a pitcher on his head would have been an unusual sight!

HYMN FOR THE DAY

The traditional Passover meal ended with the singing of this song: "Praise the Lord all you nations . . . .The stone the builders rejected has become the corner stone." After singing a hymn, Jesus and His disciples left and went to the Garden of Gethsemane. It was there that Jesus was arrested.

LAMB OF GOD

The lamb eaten in the Passover meal represented the blood spread on the doorway to protect the family from the angel of death. When Jesus died, He took the place of the Passover lamb forever.

HE DIED FOR YOU

Matthew 27; Mark 15

JESUS' BIRTH BROUGHT GREAT joy to people. His miracles brought healing. Yet Jesus understood that His whole life was a preparation for the time when He would give His life as payment for the sins of the world. As Jesus was eating His last supper with friends, the disciple named Judas left. He told officials that they would soon find Jesus in the Garden of Gethsemane on the Mount of Olives. It didn't take them long to make their move. After a hurried trial and the consent of Pilate, the Roman governor, Jesus was led away to be crucified.

THE CROWN

The thorns twisted into the crown that the soldiers mockingly crushed on Jesus' head may have been what is now called the Christ Thorn. The plant has extremely long, sharp thorns—much longer than rosebush thorns.

GOOD TO BE ROMAN
Crucifixion was one of the most torturous punishments known to mankind—so cruel that it was done only to slaves and criminals. Roman citizens were almost never crucified.

THE TEMPLE CURTAIN

At the moment Jesus died, something incredible was happening at the Temple. The curtain that separated the Holy of Holies from the rest of the Temple was torn in two from top to bottom. A Jewish historian named Josephus reports that the curtain was about four inches thick and so strong that a pair of horses couldn't pull it apart. But God tore it apart to show that people no longer had to be separated from God. Anyone can go into God's presence anytime and all of the time through Jesus!

THE MARK OF A PRISONER

The prisoner's crime was usually hung on a sign around his neck as he walked to the crucifixion site: "robber," "murderer," "led a revolt." The sign on the cross above Jesus' head was different. It said "The King of the Jews" in Hebrew, Latin, and Greek.

THE CROSS

The condemned man was fastened to the cross by nails or ropes. Often he would have a seat or peg for his feet to reduce the pressure on the arms and prolong the agony. In order to gasp a quick breath, he had to push up on his feet enough to relax his chest cavity.

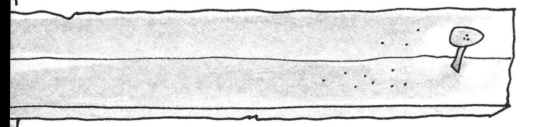

SCOURGING

Before the prisoner was hung on the cross, he was stripped of his clothes and "scourged." A scourge was a leather whip with several leather "tails." Fastened to the end of each tail was a piece of sharp metal, bone, or rock. Many prisoners died from these scourgings.

HE IS RISEN!

THE DISCIPLES COULDN'T UNDERSTAND what Mary and the other women were talking about. Their words were confusing, but there was no mistaking the joy on their faces. After spending the Sabbath in mourning, Peter and the others didn't know what to think. The women had shown up with an unbelievable story. They said they had just talked to Jesus. Soon the disciples would talk to Him, too, and they would see the greatest miracle of all. *Jesus was alive forevermore!*

A FAMILY AFFAIR

The tomb Jesus was placed in was carved out of the limestone hills around Jerusalem. Each tomb had several chambers, depending on how many people were in the family. The stone in front of the tomb was shaped like a large, heavy wheel. It sealed the tomb, but it could be reopened later.

ROLLED AWAY

The stone was rolled away so the disciples could see that Jesus had risen—not so that Jesus could get out. With His glorified body, the stone could not have stopped Him.

THE LORD'S DAY

For the Jewish people Saturday had always been the Sabbath, which means "day of rest." Soon, however, early Christians began to worship on Sunday. They called it "the Lord's day"—the day when Jesus rose from the dead. Sunday was the day the risen Jesus made most of His appearances to the disciples and the day the Holy Spirit was given at Pentecost.

PLACES TO GO...

Jesus appeared to His disciples and others many times during the 40 days between His resurrection and the time He ascended to heaven.

In Galilee:

• on the mountain

• by the Sea of Galilee where the disciples ate breakfast

In or near Jerusalem:

• to Mary Magdalene near the tomb

• to the other women

• to Peter

• to ten disciples (without Thomas)

• to 11 disciples (with Thomas)

• to two disciples on the Emmaus road

• to many people when He ascended to heaven

To 500 people:

• Paul mentions this appearance in 1 Corinthians 15:6. Five hundred people is quite a crowd to testify to Jesus' resurrection! And most of them were still alive when Paul wrote his letter to the Corinthians nearly 25 years later.

To Paul:

• It wasn't just a vision that Paul saw on the road to Damascus. It was the risen Christ.

COOL STUFF JESUS COULD DO AFTER HIS RESURRECTION

When Jesus first appeared after He rose from the dead, the disciples were afraid. They thought He was a ghost! But He wasn't.

Jesus could walk through doors and walls. He surprised the disciples this way.

He could appear and disappear whenever He wanted. Yet He had a real body, complete with scars from the cross—just ask Thomas!

Jesus could eat food. He ate broiled fish with the disciples to show them that He was real.

CAREER DAY!

PEOPLE MADE THEIR LIVING IN MANY WAYS IN JESUS' DAY. Israel was full of farmers, bankers, physicians, and merchants. There were seamstresses, weavers, coppersmiths, pottery makers, and gardeners. Of course, we're most familiar with shepherds, carpenters, and fishermen. Some of these careers have changed a lot, but some are much the same as they were 2000 years ago.

SHEPHERD GEAR

Shepherds carried a staff, usually about six feet long, as a walking stick. They used this to guide the sheep. They also had a rod—a small club used to fight off wild animals—and a leather bag or "scrip" for food and supplies. (It was in the scrip that David put the stones to slay Goliath.)

THE GOOD SHEPHERD

Shepherds seem to have a special place in God's heart. Moses and David were shepherds. The angels told shepherds about Jesus' birth rather than city leaders. And Jesus called Himself the Good Shepherd.

EMERGENCY SEWING KIT

Broken nets were mended with a long needle-like tool. Mending nets took a long time. This is what James and John were doing when Jesus called them to follow Him.

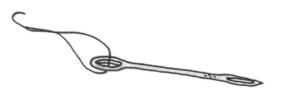

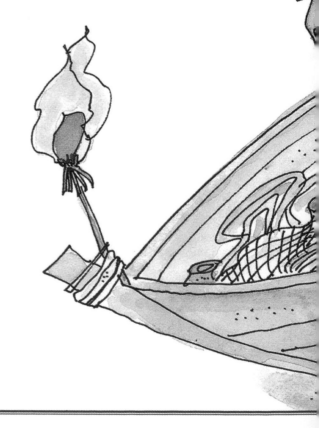

NIGHT FISHING

Before they were fishers of men, Peter, Andrew, James, and John were just regular fishermen. They often worked at night. They would use torches to draw the fish to the surface. Then they would pull long nets through the water to collect their catch.

THE PASSWORD— Ιχθύς
Early Christians used the fish as a symbol, almost like a secret code. When "fish" is spelled in the Greek language, its letters form the initials of the phrase "Jesus Christ, God's Son, Savior."

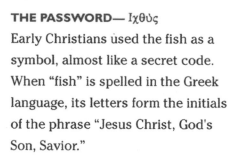

THE CARPENTER

I N JESUS' DAY, BEING A CARPENTER was hard work. It took a strong person to fashion logs into roof beams and make doors and doorframes for houses. Carpenters also built household furniture and farm tools. Plows, yokes for oxen, pitchforks, and shovels—all were made from wood and built with hand tools like bow drills and adzes.

Handsaw   chisel   saw   mallet   Axe

old workshop

STRAIGHTEN UP!

The plumb line was a string with a weight attached. It was used to make sure that whatever the carpenter was building was straight.

HAND-POWERED

A bow drill looked like a regular bow only smaller. The shaft of the drill was looped into the bowstring and made to twirl by the back-and-forth motion of the bow.

A CHISEL WITH AN ATTITUDE

The large adze was best for smoothing and flattening heavy logs.

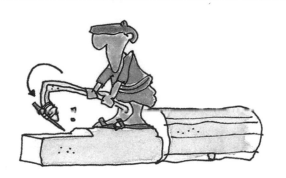

PERFECT MATCH

Different woods were good for different projects. Olive wood was best for carving. But the tough wood of the holm oak was best for making sturdy farmers' plows.

MASTER BUILDER

The Bible says that people who believe in Jesus are like parts of God's house. Jesus is the builder of that house.

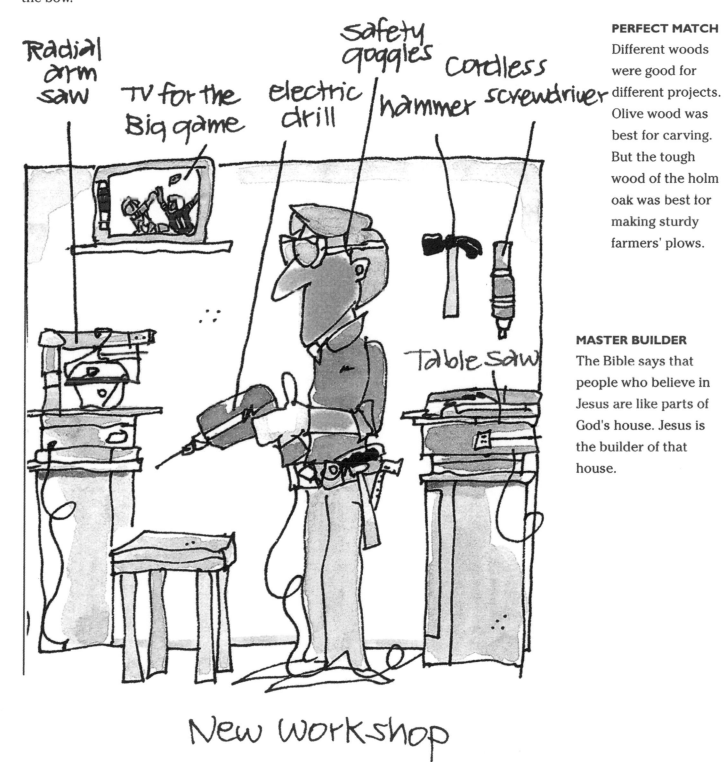

THE ROAMIN' ROMANS

Ancient Israel survived many empires, including the Assyrian, Babylonian, and Greek, but the most powerful empire arose not long before Jesus' time. It was the Roman Empire, and it spread from England all the way to central Africa. In order to be so successful, the Roman army had to recruit a lot of men. Not all of the soldiers were from Rome. If you lived in an occupied country and became a Roman soldier (called a legionnaire) you received Roman citizenship at the end of your tour of duty—a handy thing to have when your country has been invaded by Rome!

WEAKLINGS NEED NOT APPLY
Roman soldiers carried packs that weighed up to a hundred pounds. The infantry could march 20 miles a day.

PORTABLE MISSILE LAUNCHERS
One of the most powerful war engines was the catapult. It could fling a large number of javelins at enemy soldiers or hurl boulders against city walls, causing cracks and holes. Some catapults could throw a 100-pound stone, and some could throw a boulder almost half a mile. Each Roman legion had about 60 catapults. In A.D. 66 a commander named Titus laid siege against Jerusalem. He cut off supplies and pounded the walls with catapults for three and a half years before he finally broke through.

DIVISIONS OF THE ROMAN ARMY (AT FULL STRENGTH)

Just like modern armies have platoons and companies and regiments, the Roman army was divided into smaller units:

100 men = 1 century (a centurion commanded a century of men)
2 centuries = 1 maniple (200 men)
3 maniples = 1 cohort (600 men)
10 cohorts = 1 legion (6000 men)

A LEGION

At different times in its history, a Roman legion numbered 3000–6000 foot-soldiers. Soldiers didn't sign up for two years or four years like soldiers today. No way! They enlisted for 20-25 years!

ARMOR

Each Roman soldier was equipped with a large shield that was curved to protect him. It was made of wood covered with leather. Soldiers wore metal breastplates to protect their bodies and helmets made of leather or metal.

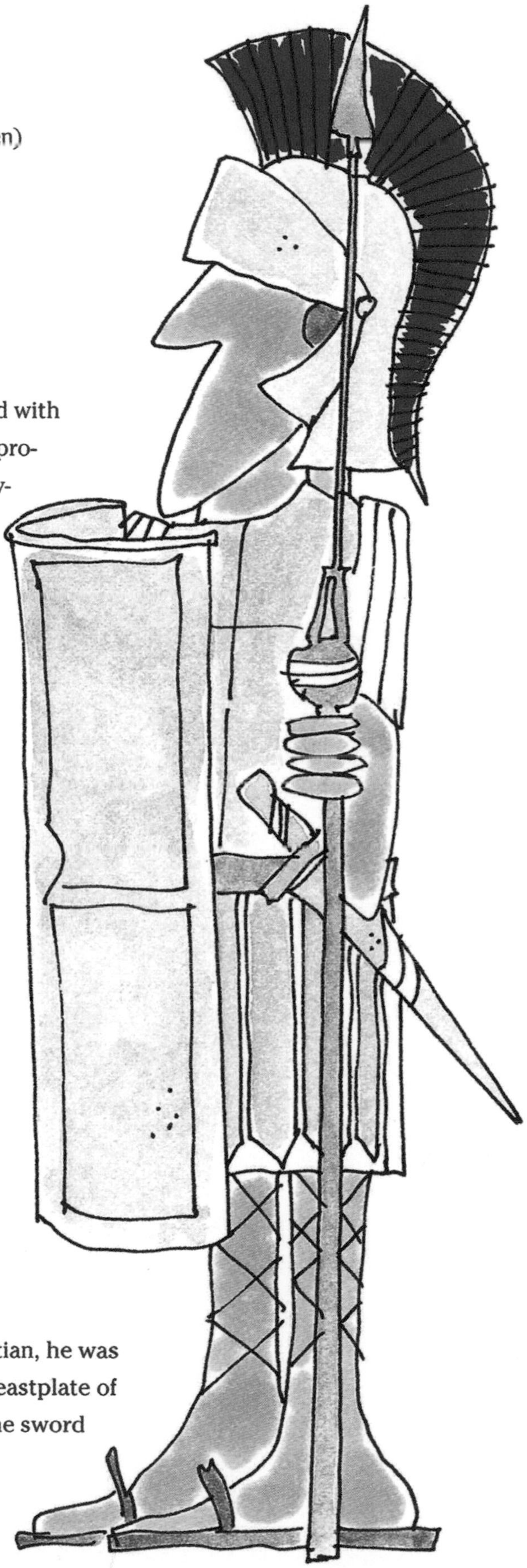

WEAPONS

A Roman soldier used a javelin, a sword, and a dagger. While still a ways off from his enemy, the soldier would throw his javelin. It would bend and become embedded in the opponent's shield. It's tough to use a shield with a seven-foot javelin sticking out of it!

A PERSONAL REPORT

When Paul wrote to the Ephesians about the warfare of the Christian, he was probably chained to a Roman soldier. When he described the "breastplate of righteousness, the shield of faith, the helmet of salvation" and "the sword of the Spirit," he would have been looking right at the armor.

PHARISEES AND SADDUCEES

During Jesus' time there were three main groups of Jewish leaders: the Pharisees, the Sadducees, and the Herodians. Many years before Jesus, these groups had been combined. The Pharisees and the Sadducees had split because they had different religious views. The Herodians broke off later, when the Roman Empire moved into Palestine. Because of their differences, these groups didn't get along too well. It was only when they began to see Jesus as a threat that they joined together to get rid of Him.

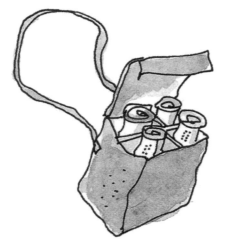

WHAT IS THIS?

A "phylactery" was a small leather box worn by Jewish men on their forehead and left arm. Inside the box were four Scriptures written out on parchment. They reminded the people to keep the Lord's commandments in their minds and near their hearts.

THE PHARISEES

The most influential group was the Pharisees. The Pharisees were mostly middle-class working people who had started out well by trying to do God's will. Unfortunately, they went too far. They were so afraid that someone might break a commandment that they developed extra rules—called "oral traditions"—to keep people in line. The Pharisees wanted everyone to think they were good and holy. But really, they were as guilty of sin as anyone else. They just couldn't see it because of their pride. They totally missed God's merciful love toward them.

WORD PICTURES

Jesus got mad at the Pharisees more then once because they expected people to keep rules that they themselves couldn't keep. He used expressive words to describe them.

brood of vipers   blind guides   hypocrites   whitewashed graves

IT'S A TRAP

The Jewish high court was called the Sanhedrin. It was made up of 70 (some say 71) Pharisees and Sadducees. The Sanhedrin condemned Jesus—but Jesus was framed! For one thing, having a trial at night was against the rules. For another, the Sanhedrin wasn't allowed to meet during feasts such as Passover.

THE HERODIANS

A less important group was the Herodians. They got their name because of their loyalty to King Herod and his sons. (Even though the Romans occupied the land, they allowed King Herod to rule Israel.) Jesus' appearance on the scene upset the Herodians' political plans.

THE SADDUCEES

Most of the Sadducees were wealthy landowners. They were very influential in the Sanhedrin. However, they were not popular with the common people. The Sadducees were very strict about keeping the law, but they did not believe in the Pharisees' added rules. They also didn't believe in a resurrection after death. Jesus made a special point of teaching them that there is a resurrection.

HEROD'S TEMPLE

King Herod was from the country of Moab, so many of the Jewish people didn't trust him. To win their favor, he made the Temple in Jerusalem into a magnificent place of worship. Jesus visited the Temple often.

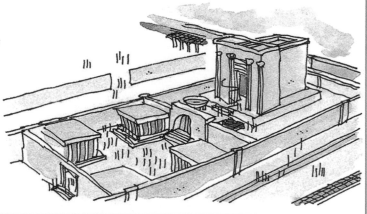

GETTING AROUND

AS WE READ ABOUT THE LAND of Israel in the Old and New Testaments and all the amazing things that happened there, it's hard to remember that the whole nation is only about 250 miles long and 70 miles at its widest point. Jesus' life and ministry has affected all of human history. Yet He never traveled farther than 85 miles from home (other than His trip to Egypt as a child). Of course, 2000 years ago, travel was more difficult, dangerous. . . and a whole lot slower.

THE GREATER ISRAEL WALK-A-THON

The main method of transportation in Jesus' time was walking. Walking from Jerusalem to Jericho, like the unfortunate man in the Good Samaritan story, was a day's journey (about 15 miles).

STORM'S A BREWIN'

Jesus and His disciples navigated the Sea of Galilee often. Others, like Paul, traveled by ship on the Mediterranean Sea. Big merchant ships were mostly Roman. In ideal conditions they could cover 55 nautical miles a day. Conditions on the Mediterranean, though, were rarely ideal. The Romans forbade sailing between November 10 and March 10. One of the two ships on which Paul was a prisoner did sail, though. It was wrecked off the coast of Malta.

PONY EXPRESS

At rest stops along the way, Roman couriers could find food and fresh mounts. The fastest riders could make about 75 miles per day. But they were no match for modern travel. The space shuttle flies at 17,500 miles per hour!

REST STOP

ALL IN A DAY'S WORK

Some wealthier citizens of Israel could afford donkeys to ride. Donkeys moved a little faster than people and could cover about 20 miles a day, without all the wear and tear on the rider.

MILES TO GO ...

Roman mile: 4850 feet
Nautical mile: 6076 feet
Standard mile: 5280 feet

PORTER ... TAKE MY BAGS

Mileposts along the Roman roads showed people how far they had traveled. But they had another use. By Roman law, soldiers could force civilians to carry their gear from one milepost to the next. That's what Jesus was talking about when He said that if someone forces you to go one mile with him, you should offer to go an extra mile!

ALL ROADS LEAD TO ROME

The Roman road system was the best in the world. It connected Rome to Europe and Egypt and beyond. It was on these roads that Paul, Silas, Barnabas, and Timothy spread the gospel through the civilized world. God used the Roman Empire's achievements to further His kingdom.

CAUTION: FLAGGER AHEAD

Roman roads were smooth and level, with drainage ditches and sometimes raised walkways.

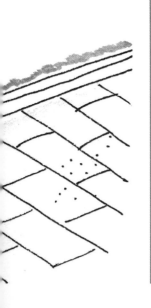

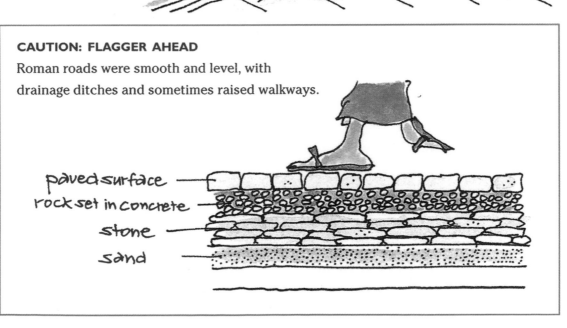

paved surface
rock set in concrete
stone
sand

HOME SWEET HOME

HOUSES IN JESUS' TIME DIDN'T HAVE DISHWASHERS (except for the kids). And no one hogged the bathroom, because there wasn't one! Of course, the more money a family had the nicer their house was. These two houses are like homes Jesus would have visited or built furniture for in His carpentry shop.

THE BUDGET MODEL

Ordinary families—like those of fishermen or tradesmen—lived in single-story dwellings made of either mud bricks or stone. Inside there were two levels: a lower one at the front where domestic animals like sheep or goats could be housed, and a second level of stone about 12-18 inches higher. Here the family cooked, ate, and slept. After the sun went down and the dinner dishes had been cleared away, the family would lay out their sleeping mats.

THE GRASS IS GREENER ...

Rooftops were used so much that Jewish law required ledges to be built around them so people wouldn't fall off. In the wet season, seeds left in the brush-and-mud roofs sprouted, and the housetops all turned green!

WE'LL LEAVE THE LIGHT ON FOR YOU

In Jesus' time, bowls of olive oil with a wick served as the main source of light in a house. Some lamps were covered to prevent spills.

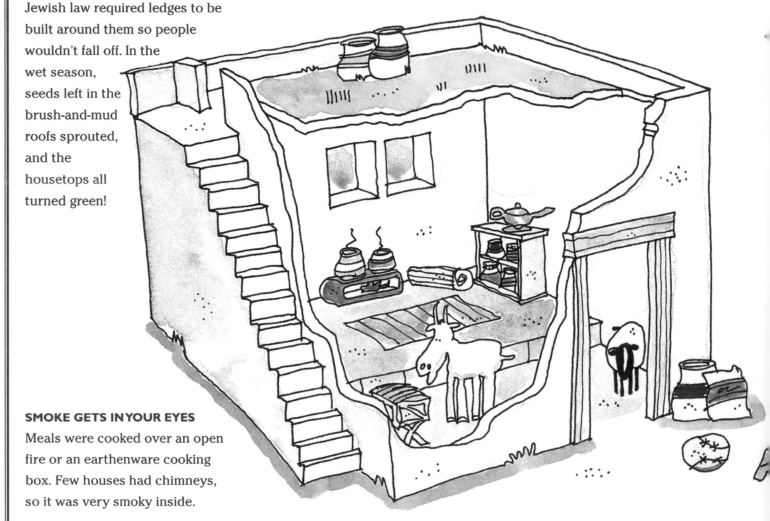

SMOKE GETS IN YOUR EYES

Meals were cooked over an open fire or an earthenware cooking box. Few houses had chimneys, so it was very smoky inside.

LUXURY LIVING

Wealthy families in Palestine often had houses that were several stories high, with open courtyards and surrounding stone walls. Inside were tiled floors and walls, water from storage cisterns, and occasionally indoor heating! Some even had bathtubs (okay, so a few had bathrooms, but not many). This is the kind of house that Zaccheus, the wealthy tax collector, probably lived in when he entertained Jesus.

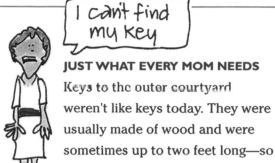

JUST WHAT EVERY MOM NEEDS

I can't find my key

Keys to the outer courtyard weren't like keys today. They were usually made of wood and were sometimes up to two feet long—so large that they were carried over the shoulder.

RICH KIDS

Children from wealthier families had puppets, dolls with movable parts and real hair, and dollhouse furniture made of pottery. Jewish children were not allowed to play with dolls because they believed it went against the commandment not to make any "graven images."

WATER

Water had to be carried from the town well.

B.C.P. (BEFORE COUCH POTATOES)

Because houses didn't have many windows, it was usually dark inside. Children spent their time playing or doing their chores outside. Many of the games that children played are still popular today: marbles, leap-frog, and games with balls and hoops. Video games were still 2000 years in the future!

PAUL'S JOURNEYS

Acts 13–28

PAUL HAD BEEN JEWISH ALL HIS LIFE. He was proud of his heritage. One day Paul, who was then called Saul, was traveling to Damascus to arrest followers of Jesus. Oh, how he hated those new Christians! He wanted to put them in jail or stone them to death. But then Jesus appeared to him on the road. Paul was a changed man after that. He spent the rest of his life as a missionary, spreading the gospel. "Gospel" means *"good news"*— the good news of Jesus. Sometimes Paul was welcomed. Sometimes he was not. But he told people about Jesus' love wherever he went.

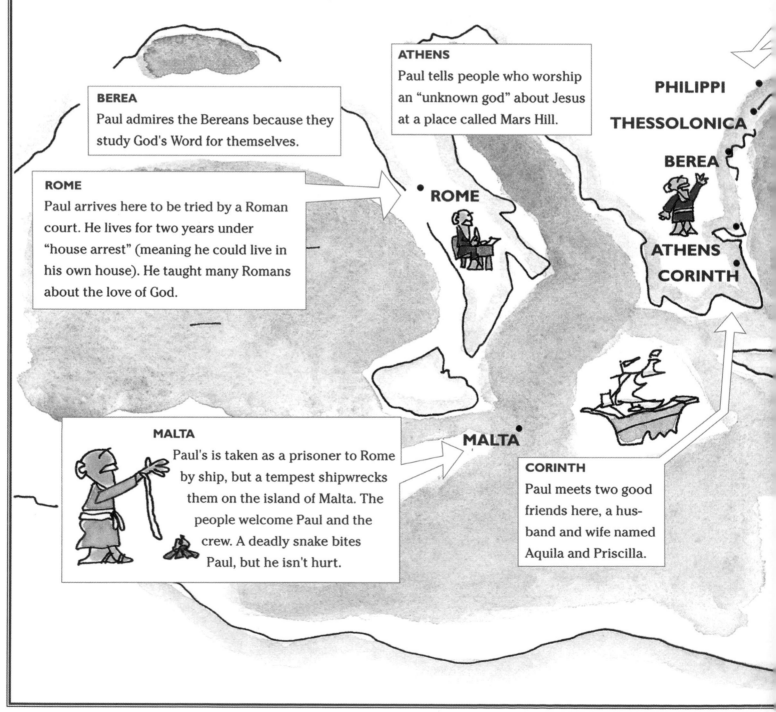

BEREA
Paul admires the Bereans because they study God's Word for themselves.

ATHENS
Paul tells people who worship an "unknown god" about Jesus at a place called Mars Hill.

PHILIPPI

THESSOLONICA

BEREA

ROME
Paul arrives here to be tried by a Roman court. He lives for two years under "house arrest" (meaning he could live in his own house). He taught many Romans about the love of God.

ROME

ATHENS

CORINTH

MALTA
Paul's is taken as a prisoner to Rome by ship, but a tempest shipwrecks them on the island of Malta. The people welcome Paul and the crew. A deadly snake bites Paul, but he isn't hurt.

MALTA

CORINTH
Paul meets two good friends here, a husband and wife named Aquila and Priscilla.

PHILIPPI

Paul and Silas are thrown into jail for preaching the gospel. At midnight they sing hymns of praise. A huge earthquake breaks the doors and walls of the prison wide open. Instead of escaping, Paul and Silas tell the jailer about Jesus. He becomes a Christian.

TROAS

Paul preaches late into the night. A young man named Eutychus falls asleep, drops from his seat on a third-story window sill, and dies. God brings him back to life—and Paul keeps on preaching until dawn.

LYSTRA

God uses Paul to heal a crippled man, so the people think Paul and Barnabas are gods. They want to worship them. But Paul will have none of it! Then enemies from Iconium and Antioch show up and get the crowd to stone Paul, leaving him for dead. What a day!

ANTIOCH

Followers of Jesus were first called Christians in Antioch.

TROAS

ICONIUM •

LYSTRA •

EPHESUS •

ANTIOCH •

IN THE SPOTLIGHT

On the road to Damascus, Jesus appeared to Paul in a great flood of light that knocked Paul to the ground. He was blind for three days, until a Christian prayed for him.

CYPRUS

CYPRUS

A magician tries to confuse Paul's message, but the Lord strikes the magician blind.

DAMASCUS •

EPHESUS

Paul stays here for about two years until the followers of a false goddess named Diana become so upset that they cause a riot. They pour into an outdoor theater that holds 25,000 people!

FREQUENT FLYER MILES

Q: How many miles did Paul travel on his three missionary journeys and his final journey to Rome?
A: About 9200. That's like walking, riding a donkey, and traveling by ship from Canada to the tip of South America!

KIDS IN THE BIBLE

J ESUS LOVES KIDS! One day when He was teaching, parents started bringing their children to Him. The disciples became upset. They tried to shoo them away. But Jesus told the disciples to stop. "Don't keep them from coming to Me!" He said. Instead He gathered the children into His arms and blessed them.

ANGELS WATCHIN' OVER YOU

God gives children angels to watch over them. And Jesus told adults to be careful how they treat kids. He said, "Make sure you don't despise one of these little ones, for their angels in heaven are always looking into the face of My Father" (Matthew 18:10).

YOU ARE A GIFT!

Remind your parents every once in a while. The Bible says, "Behold, children are a gift of the Lord; the fruit of the womb is a reward" (Psalm 127:3).

TIMOTHY studied the Scripture from the time he was young (2 Timothy 3:15). He grew up to become a pastor in the city of Ephesus.

SAMUEL learned at a young age to listen for God's voice and obey it. He became a prophet.

JAIRUS' DAUGHTER was healed by Jesus.

JOSIAH was eight years old when he became a good king.

A LITTLE SLAVE GIRL who served Naaman's wife told Naaman that Elijah could heal his leprosy.

A NARROW ESCAPE

Once there were two women who had babies. One of the babies died. The mother of the dead baby switched the children. When the real mother discovered this, she brought the matter to King Solomon. King Solomon said, "Let's cut the baby in two and give half to each of you. That ought to settle things." This horrified the real mother, who cried, "No! Let her have the baby." Then Solomon knew that she was the real mother and gave the child back to her.

KIDS PRAISED JESUS!

When Jesus came into the Temple, threw out the money-changers, and healed the blind and lame, a group of children started shouting, "Hosanna!" This upset the religious leaders, but the kids had a blast and Jesus loved it (Matthew 21:15).

THE PRODIGAL SON

ran away from home, but his father still loved him. He threw a party to welcome him back.

CHILDREN IN THE TEMPLE

were some of the first to praise Jesus.

THE WIDOW'S SON

Jesus brought this boy back to life at his funeral.

DELIVERY BOY

This boy's lunch fed 5000 men and their families.

JOHN THE BAPTIST

leaped in his mother's womb when he heard Jesus' mom say hello. He grew up to tell people that God's kingdom was near. Jesus was coming!

MEPHIBOSHETH

was only five years old when his nurse dropped him and he became lame. Years later, King David found Mephibosheth. "Come eat at my table" he told him. "Don't be afraid. Your father and I were best friends. We made an agreement that I would take care of his family." The agreement was called a covenant.

BABY MOSES

took his first trip in a basket!

AN AMAZING BOOK

THE BIBLE IS GOD'S BOOK for all time. God loved people, so He put it into their hearts to write down His words on paper. He did this because He wanted you to know Him like a wonderful Father. And He wanted you to meet His Son, Jesus, who is the best friend anyone could ever have.

WHO WROTE IT?

About 40 different men wrote the 66 books of the Bible. Moses wrote the first book some 3500 years ago. The apostle John wrote the last book about 1900 years ago.

COPY CATS

The books of the Old Testament were preserved by Jewish scribes. These specially trained men copied the words on animal skins called parchment. The scribes had to count each letter to make sure they were all there!

HOW CAN WE KNOW IT'S TRUE?

Jesus believed the Old Testament. And He told people they should believe everything the prophets had said (Luke 24:25). Jesus and other writers in the New Testament quote the Old Testament about *600* times.

EARLY COMICS

About 700 years ago, wood-block Bible stories were invented. They were like our comic books. Each one had an illustration of a New Testament story, along with a scene from the Old Testament that taught the same lesson. They were called Poor Man's Bibles because they didn't cost much and people didn't have to know how to read to understand them.

THE COST OF MATERIALS

It took 25 sheep to make parchment for 200 pages of Bible text.

LONDON BRIDGE IS FALLING DOWN ...

In the Middle Ages, a copy of the Bible cost more to produce than two arches of the London Bridge!

CHAINS

Handwritten copies of the Bible were so valuable that they were chained to their place in the church—like pens in the Post Office!

SPREADING THE WORD

It wasn't until the printing press came into use in Europe that the Bible could be produced at a price common people could afford. The first mass-produced Bible was printed by Johannes Gutenberg in Mainz, Germany in 1456.

why would
someone
give you
his
sandal
in ancient
Israel?
page 33

THE
AWESOME
BOOK
of BIBLE
FACTS

Copyright © 1994 by Harvest House Publishers
Eugene, Oregon 97402

ISBN 978-1-56507-225-1

Manufactured in China

14 15 16 17 18 19 20 / FC / 20 19 18 17 16 15